"DEAR FATHER"/"DEAR SON"

John D. Rockefeller and John D. Rockefeller, Jr., at the Park Avenue Baptist Church, New York City, May 3, 1925. All photographs in this book are courtesy of the Rockefeller Archive Center, Pocantico Hills, N.Y.

"Dear Father"/ "Dear Son"

Correspondence of John D. Rockefeller and John D. Rockefeller, Jr.

Edited by
JOSEPH W. ERNST

FORDHAM UNIVERSITY PRESS
IN COOPERATION WITH
ROCKEFELLER ARCHIVE CENTER

New York
1994

Rockefeller Archive Center is a
division of The Rockefeller University
LC 94–7702
ISBN 0–8232–1559–8

Library of Congress Cataloging-in-Publication Data

"Dear father"/"dear son" : correspondence of John D. Rockefeller and John D. Rockefeller, Jr. / edited by Joseph W. Ernst.
p. cm.
Includes bibliographical references.
ISBN 0–8232–1559–8
1. Rockefeller, John D. (John Davison), 1839–1937—Correspondence. 2. Rockefeller, John D. (John Davison), 1874–1960—Correspondence. 3. Capitalists and financiers—United States—Correspondence. 4. Industrialists—United States—Correspondence. 5. Philanthropists—United States—Correspondence. I. Ernst, Joseph W., 1923——. II. Rockefeller, John D. (John Davison), 1839–1937. III. Rockefeller, John D. (John Davison), 1874–1960.
CT275.R75A4 1994
338.7'6223382'092—dc20
[B] 94–7702
CIP

Printed in the United States of America

For my wife, Helen,
my daughter, Elizabeth,
and my three sons, Stephen, Christopher, and Jonathan

CONTENTS

PREFACE

What did it mean to be "rich as Rockefeller"?

John D. Rockefeller, Jr., believed that every right implied a responsibility; every opportunity, an obligation; every possession, a duty. How he shared these ideals with his father is revealed in this short compilation of letters they exchanged over 50 years.

Historians, journalists, and other commentators have offered differing interpretations of what it meant to be a Rockefeller. There were over 200 magazine articles and more than 60 books written on this father and son between 1896 and 1990. Some had access to this correspondence, others did not. Among those who did not were Ida Tarbell, who published her works on John D. Rockefeller and the Standard Oil Company in 1904 and 1905; Henry Demarest Lloyd, who published in 1894; and Matthew Josephson, who published in 1934 and 1938.[1]

Allan Nevins was the first to have access to these letters. He and his researcher read over 1,000 letters which had been selected from the family files by John D. Rockefeller, Jr. Nevins quoted key sections of the letters as he developed his 1940 vision of Rockefeller in the heroic age of American enterprise. Most of the same quotes appear in his revised 1953 version of the biography of Rockefeller, industrialist and philanthropist.[2]

Raymond B. Fosdick's biography of Rockefeller Junior, published in 1956, was the second study based extensively on the same 1,000 letters. These letters, removed from their original places in the files and organized chronologically, constitute a separate file series in the family archives at the Rockefeller Archive Center.[3]

These biographies provided other authors secondary access to this series. The letters have been quoted to support the differing views of the several authors. Grace Goulder, concentrating on Rockefeller Senior as a citizen of Cleveland, found a rich vein of early Cleveland history. Alvin Moscow traced the thread of stewardship and philanthropy into the third generation from the letters. Peter Collier and David Horowitz discovered the seeds of a conspiracy to control the United States, if not the world.[4]

Ralph and Muriel Hidy had access to the letters for their history of Standard Oil of New Jersey. David Freeman Hawke used them for his concise look at Rockefeller Senior as the consummate businessman, while Peter Johnson and Jack Harr found in the letters the family values and setting which fostered the philanthropies of John D. Rockefeller 3rd.[5]

Thus, bits and pieces of the 1,000 letters have appeared in print over the past 50 years. This filial relationship has been used to prove diametrically opposing views of the men and of the institutions they established.

The letters are presented here without comment; they speak for themselves. No motives have been assigned, no long-range planning has been attributed to passing words of the moment. Only people, places, events, and things not known from the context of the letters have been identified. Only typing errors have been corrected.

Every father and every son might hope for the love and understanding displayed in these letters. This love, this understanding, and these commitments were not contingent on being "rich as Rockefeller."

Notes

1. Ida M. Tarbell, *History of the Standard Oil Company* (New York: Phillips & Company, 1904); Henry Demarest Lloyd, *Wealth Against Commonwealth* (New York: Harper & Brothers, 1894); Matthew Josephson, *The Robber Barons* (New York: Harcourt Brace, 1938).
2. Allan Nevins, *John D. Rockefeller: The Heroic Age of American Enterprise* (New York: Charles Scribner's Sons, 1940) and *Study in Power: John D. Rockefeller, Industrialist and Philanthropist* (New York: Charles Scribner's Sons, 1953).
3. Raymond B. Fosdick, *John D. Rockefeller, Jr., A Portrait* (New York: Harper & Brothers, 1956).
4. Grace Goulder, *John D. Rockefeller: The Cleveland Years* (Cleveland: Western Reserve Historical Society, 1972); Alvin Moscow, *The Rockefeller Inheritance* (Garden City, N.Y.: Doubleday & Company, 1977); Peter Collier and David Horowitz, *The Rockefellers: An American Dynasty* (New York: Holt, Rinehart and Winston, 1976).

5. Ralph Hidy and Muriel E. Hidy, *Pioneering in Big Business: History of Standard Oil Company (New Jersey), 1882–1911* (New York: Harper & Brothers, 1955); David Freeman Hawke, *John D.: The Founding Father of the Rockefellers* (New York: Harper & Row, 1980); John E. Harr and Peter J. Johnson, *The Rockefeller Century* (New York: Charles Scribner's Sons, 1988).

THE LETTERS

On November 17, 1887, John D. Rockefeller, Jr., 13, wrote a letter to his father, 48, who was in New York City. Rockefeller Junior and his mother, Laura Spelman Rockefeller, were spending the winter at Forest Hill, the Rockefeller home in Cleveland. The son had been ailing and his parents decided that the park-like environment of Forest Hill would accelerate his recovery. The following selection of letters exchanged between father and son begins with Rockefeller Senior's reply to that letter.

26 Broadway
New York
November 19, 1887

Dear Johnny:

Yours, 17th, just at hand, and so happy to hear from you and that you and your little Mother are doing so nicely in the quiet of the woods. Am in the midst of hard battles today, but getting on nicely, and looking forward to dropping in upon you sometime before long. It is not likely I can do so, however, for Thanksgiving, which I regret. I have been called to Washington, but did not heed the summons, but hold myself in readiness to go at a moment's notice. Mr. Brewster and several others go over to be there Monday morning. Think your decision right in reference to the shed. Everything going on nicely at home. Old Mr. Hubbell, now 77 years of age, came down this morning. He is the same dear good Methodist man he used to be. Stayed with us at the table and drank coffee and ate cakes and syrup. Went over the house and enjoyed it much. Gave him an order for a bedstead for the spare room. His price will be several hundred dollars less than Pottier and I presume the bedstead will be as good or better than Pottier's, and we know the beds are unsurpassed. Should this not be satisfactory to Mamma, we can have the bedstead sent to Forest Hill for next year, as we have talked of having new ones there. We like the appearance of the new man and think he will do well. Everything goes on smoothly in the house. You say you are not lonely. That is not the case with me. I am however doing the best I can, and the rest are all doing remarkably well.

I have not written to Mama but telegraphed every day. Been so busy and knew numbers of letters were written from the house. She will get all the news. Business affairs going nicely. With much love to you and Mama and great appreciation of the beautiful letter you wrote me.

Your loving
Father.

Mr. John D. Rockefeller, Jr.
Forest Hill,
East Cleveland, O.

By 1887 the John D. Rockefeller family had two homes in Cleveland and one in New York City. Rockefeller purchased 997 Euclid Avenue, Cleveland, in 1868. It was a two-story Victorian home. John D. Rockefeller, Jr. was born in this house on January 29, 1874. The second Cleveland home, Forest Hill, eventually a 700-acre estate, was acquired in 1878. The house, a three-story building, was originally built as a health resort. Over the years Rockefeller developed the property with a farm, two lakes for skating and swimming, a racetrack for his horses, bicycle trails, and a nine-hole golf course. The house burned down in December 1917. In the 1930s part of the estate was developed into single-family homes, an apartment complex, and a shopping area. The rest was given to the public as a park.

Between 1877 and 1884, when in New York, Rockefeller and his family had rooms in the Buckingham Hotel, between 49th and 50th Streets on Fifth Avenue. In October 1884 he purchased 4 West 54th Street, a furnished four-story brownstone house built in l865–66. He made few changes in the house during the four decades he lived there.

After 1877 the family normally spent the months from May to October in Cleveland and October to May in New York. However, Junior and his mother, Laura Spelman Rockefeller, spent the winter of 1887–88 at Forest Hill, as Junior was not in the best of health. This separation led to the earliest surviving correspondence between Rockefeller and his son.

In the fall of 1887 and the spring of 1888 Rockefeller and other trustees of the Standard Oil Trust testified before the U.S. House Committee investigating trusts. Benjamin Brewster was one of the original trustees.

Pottier was a highly regarded New York manufacturer and retailer of furniture.

---

26 Broadway
New York
November 28th 1887

Dear John:

Yours, of the 22nd, duly received. Excuse delay in answering. Have also your telegram of today for the cutter, and will attend to it tomorrow morning. I assume you want the one to carry two persons. I had a pleasant time in Washington. It is a beautiful city. The weather was mild and lovely. After receiving my testimony they did not wish any other although they had subpoenaed eight of us. We feel very well about the experience over there. The New York World hasn't any further ammunition in this direction, is now going back to its first love, the Buffalo suit, trying to rake up something against us. Had a delightful Sunday at home yesterday. Feeling well and ready for business. Looking forward with pleasure to seeing you the last of this week.

Concur in your decision about painting the storm doors. You and Mother will surely have your own way in all these affairs, what's the use of my saying a word. You are monarch of all you survey.

Your loving
Father

Forest Hill
East Cleveland, Ohio

In 1881 there was an explosion at the Buffalo Lubricating Company, a competitor of the Standard Oil Company. Three Standard Oil officials were indicted for alleged criminal actions. Although their indictments were eventually squashed by the courts, the explosion was frequently cited as an example of Standard's business tactics. The New York World *was one newspaper that kept the issue before the public. The entire affair is treated in Allan Nevins,* John D. Rockefeller: The Heroic Age in American Enterprise *(New York: Charles Scribner's Sons, 1940), II, pp. 76–79.*

Forest Hill
East Cleveland, Ohio
January 15,1888

Dear Father,

Your letters received and greatly enjoyed. We have had some skating although nothing as good as when you were with us. The first part of the week we cut ice for a day or two and the next day Mr. Sinclair flooded a piece along in front of the standpipe,—and by the way they have fixed the standpipe and all we want now is water to fill it.

Thursday the Dowlings came out and skated. Friday at noon it thawed a good deal and froze during the night so that yesterday we had pretty good skating. But the ridges where we piled the snow when you were here have not melted and they make it rather bad. We are going to try and break them up so that they will melt. Yesterday afternoon Mrs. Biggar and her children came out and skated. She skates very well.

Last night it rained a good deal and then froze so that today the horses—although they were quite sharp—could hardly stand up. Euclid is just one sheet of ice and we had to go all the way in the car tracks, even on Prospect. I only saw one or two carriages on Euclid. I think we were the only persons that came to church in a carriage.

Mother says that Mr. Chase and Amy came to her after church and wanted to know if she was hurt from her fall off the sled when they were out. Mr. C said he would like to try skating again.

Mother gets along nicely and skates with me alone, without the chair. She enjoys it greatly. Mrs. Moore put on skates for a minute the other day but she said her ankles felt as if they were carrying tons, they were so weak.

I have driven the nigh horse in the team with Ed lately and like him ever so much. Ed drove the other one single the other day and said that he went very well indeed.

Mother wants to know if you will find out if any thing is being done about the telephone wire from the office to Forest Hill.

Love to all,
John

26 B'way
New York

Mr. Sinclair was the superintendent of the Forest Hill estate. The Reverend George T. Dowling was minister of the Euclid Avenue Baptist Church. It came to be known as the Rockefeller church. Mrs. Biggar was the wife of Dr. Hamilton F. Biggar, homeopathic physician and Rockefeller's personal physician. A frequent golf partner, he traveled with the family to Europe; his grandson Benjamin T. Gilbert married Rockefeller's granddaughter Madeline E. Prentice. Mrs. Moore was housekeeper at Forest Hill. The Chases were friends and members of the Euclid Avenue Baptist Chruch.

26 Broadway
January 20th 1888

My Dear Son:

We all welcomed yours of the 15th. Were very pleased to hear of your daily experience, and hope both you and Mother will be much better for this quiet country life. I am glad you know about it. It carries me back to my boyhood days. I am having a pair of shoes made to lace up. I am told they support the ankles better. I will bring them with me. Please tell Mother that everything is being done that can be in reference to the telephone wire to Forest Hill. A new route is desired and the effort to secure it makes a little delay. Aunty and I went to the Harlem River this morning with Flash and Midnight in a new cutter which cost $300. Very extravagant I know, but the sleighing is so good could not resist the temptation to buy it and hope to get the worth of our money. I drove four times day before yesterday and three times yesterday making an aggregate in the two days of about eighty miles. Don't you think I am an enthusiastic youth? I am looking forward with great pleasure to seeing you next week but may not leave until Friday.

Lovingly,
Your Father

Forest Hill
East Cleveland, Ohio

Aunty was Lucy Spelman, Laura's sister. Flash and Midnight were a pair of black gelding trotters. Rockefeller enjoyed driving and racing and often raced against his neighbors down Enclid Avenue as well as on the track he had at Forest Hill.

Forest Hill
June 1st 91

My dear Son:

We are just in receipt of your telegram in reference to Edith's book—Hope you had a pleasant Sabbath. It has been delightful here since we came. We all feel the letting down process, changing from the Seaboard to the interior, but it is delightful, and I trust it will be the thing best calculated to give us all health and strength.

I suppose Mama or the girls have written you in reference to the Sunday School, and it was not my purpose to write you a letter, but I wanted to tell you about answering my telegrams—Preface your answers with "telegram received" and they will go free just the same as mine, under my frank. Take the best care of your health. Enjoy the society of your friends in the country and telegraph at once if there is anything you want me to do for you.

We all unite in love.

Your affectionate,
Father

4 W 54th Street
New York

Edith Rockefeller McCormick was Senior's fourth daughter. She was born on August 31, 1872, and died on August 25, 1932.

Forest Hill
Sunday
February 14, 1892

My dear Father,

When you write Mr. Sinclair, please make it very plain that Edward is to have complete charge of the work horses. Mr. S. and Edward had a discussion about a horse that has been sick. All the teamsters think him well enough to work, and Edward told Mr. S.—so whereupon he replied that he did not care what any of them said he knew more than all of them put together. I only mention this that you may leave no doubt in Mr. S.'s mind about who is to have charge of the horses. Yesterday morning the thermometer was 10°, and the skating splendid, so Grace and I went up after breakfast and she skated two hours and enjoyed it much. In the afternoon there were nearly fifty people skating, none of our friends, however, and in the evening they had a fine time there.

When I cut down a hollow tree the other day a cat ran out of it. It has since occurred to me that that must have been a catalpa tree.

I want to tell you how deeply I appreciate the trouble and expense you have incurred in order that I might stay here this winter, and how sincerely grateful I am to you.

I thank God for such a Mother and such a Father as he has given me, and pray that as the days and years go by I can prove my appreciation to them for all they have done for me or at least to show them my gratitude.

I have been told that there is an article in the East End Signal thanking you in behalf of the young people of Collamer for so kindly allowing them to enjoy the skating on the lake.

I will procure it and sent it to you. Edward tells me that a number of the boys wanted to ask you to keep the lake cleared for them after you went away, and spoke to him about it. Another case of "bronze" as you term it.

I hope you had a pleasant journey and reached New York

none the worse for your visit. I cannot tell you how much I enjoyed having you and Mother here.

Lovingly,
John

26 Broadway
New York

---

26 Broadway
New York
February 17, 1892

Dear John:

Yours of the 14th was duly received yesterday, and mama and I read it as we were riding in the brougham, and both greatly enjoyed it from every point of view. Be assured the appreciation you show is ample payment for all we have ever tried to do for you, and I have not words to express our gratitude for what you show us in your daily life, and for the hope you give us for the future time when our turn comes for us to lean more on you.

I wrote Mr. Sinclair, as follows, on Monday of this week,

"I desire to have Edward take full charge of the farm barns and buildings, also the horses and the work centering there. I supposed this was understood last June."

We had a very pleasant journey home, arriving a little late. The weather has been delightful here and the skating good, though only a few friends with us to enjoy it. We are all feeling quite well, and our pleasure would be so much enhanced if you could be with us: but we much prefer you should do as you are doing, believing it to be best for you, and consequently for us all.

Both sermons on Sunday were excellent, and the work goes on prosperously.

I have made some fine loans since returning, and engaged in some new business projects which are promising.

Lovingly,
Your Father

Forest Hill
Cleveland, Ohio

The Rockefellers attended the Fifth Avenue Baptist Church when in New York. W. H. P. Faunce was the minister in 1892. He later became president of Brown University.

---

11 Slater Hall
Brown University
September 24, 1893

My dear Father,

My funds are about exhausted, and I write to ask you if you will kindly send me $100.

There are many little bills in connection with furnishing my rooms, which I can as well pay as not, thus saving you the trouble of these small items. Of course, the larger bills for furniture I will send to you as you kindly said I might.

We are getting on here famously, and all enjoy it immensely. The fellows are more than kind to us, and especially helpful to us just at this time when we need directions and advice. I presume we have met over twenty five men belonging to the Alpha Delta Phi society and have already pledged our selves to join that society. Lefferts and I had a slight experience of hazing the other night, but nothing to speak of. However, after the fellows left our room they visited others of the freshmen, and got so frolicsome with them, that as a result five have been suspended, and of that number a couple will probably be expelled.

President Andrews is perfectly fine, and wonderfully fitted for his position. He talks to the fellows so plainly, and about matters which come very near home, and yet does it in such a nice way that no one feels the least bit hurt. Our class is the largest which had ever entered college, and numbers about 175. Grandmother will be interested to know that there are three colored men in the class. We had a class prayer-meeting the other afternoon, and you would have been much pleased with the spirit exhibited. Before the meeting was over, all the men from the three other class prayer meetings came in in single file singing "Blessed be the tie that binds", and while they sang they walked through one line of seats and then another, and every man of them shook hands with every man in our class. Then they all stood around, and one of them prayed, and then said a few words about the responsibility resting upon each of us, and the amount of good that a band of fellows could do if they would stand together. It was really very inspiring.

We have a splendid boarding house, at least Ev and I have. The board is $8 a week and neither Lefferts or Archie can stand that, so they have to go elsewhere.

I hope everything is going well at Forest Hill, and that you are not working too hard. How pleasant it will be if you can get into the Tarrytown house this fall for a few weeks.

With much love to all, I am affectionately,

John

26 Broadway
New York

Junior entered Brown University in the fall of 1893. Among his close friends at Brown were Lefferts Dashiell, Everett Colby, and Archibald McClave. E. Benjamin Andrews, president of Brown in 1893, supported William Jennings Bryan in 1896. Junior took his course in "Practical Ethics."

Grandmother Lucy Henry Spelman and her husband, Harvey B. Spelman, were active abolitionists. Spelman College in Atlanta was named in their honor.

In 1893 Rockefeller began buying land and houses in Pocantico

Hills, North Tarrytown, New York. The first house purchased was called Kykuit and the name was used for the stone mansion built on the site after the original wooden house burned down. Eventually Rockefeller owned over 3,500 acres. The estate was the principal country home for him, his son, and four grandsons. Kykuit has been given to the National Trust for Historic Preservation.

Forest Hill
Cleveland, Ohio
September 27, 1893

My Dear John.

We were all very happy to receive your first long letter on entering upon your college life at Brown—It seems a very auspicious beginning and on reading it I was confirmed respecting our decision for Brown instead of Yale—There are men enough and I judge a good class and the moral and religious tone seem of the best, besides how very cordially they receive you and your friends. I have forwarded your letter to your mother. We all read it over and over again with pleasure—Glad to know your arrangments seem to be so favorable for the beginning—

You must have good nourishing food at all times and plenty of it—You cant work without you eat—

If you decide at any time you would like your riding horse we will send him to you—

You must have plenty of exercise in the open air. We could send an extra one for the use of your friends if you so desire—

We intend to go to New York next Friday and Uncle Rudd will accompany us—Mother arrived in Philadelphia Tuesday morning after a pleasant safe journey—

We cut down some more trees and made a decided improvement—the prominent oak in the group south west of the house, also maple near chestnut just below it and the tall thin maple down in front—

The weather is delightful—We pass the time very pleasantly and all join in love.

Your Father

No 11 Slater Hall,
Providence, R.I.

William Cullen Rudd married Mary Ann Rockefeller, John D. Rockefeller's sister. He was president of Chandler and Rudd, a Cleveland grocery and specialty store.

Providence, R.I.
January 27, 1894

My dear Father,

Again I am writing for money. I fear you will think me unsatisfiable in that line. There is however a continual outgo up here and I hope a corresponding income with you.

Your check for $25 I sent to the President for the poor student about whom I spoke to you. The fellow himself does not know where the money came from, but Dr. A sent me a note of thanks and I in turn sent you his thanks as well as my own.

We are all very happy that Dr. Andrews is not going to leave although of course I feel sorry for Dr. Harper and the University.

We are having a heavy snow storm, almost a foot of snow has fallen and travel is much impeded.

I was glad to learn from Mother's letter that you had a pleasant time in Morristown, and are feeling better.

Please send me $100 when it is convenient.
With love from

John

26 Broadway
New York

Dr. William Rainey Harper was the first president of the University of Chicago.

Home
4 West 54th St.
New York
January 26, 1895

My Dear Son:

I enclose check to your order for Twenty-one dollars, for your twenty first birthday, being one for each year.

It would be very pleasant if we could all spend the day together at home, but I think under the circumstances, it is better for you to remain at college as you have been obliged to be away from your work so much of late.

I cannot tell you how much happiness we all have in you, and how much we are looking forward to, and relying on you for in the future.

We are grateful beyond measure for your promise and for the confidence your life inspires in us, not only, but in all your friends and acquaintances and this is of more value than all earthly possessions.

We all join in the hope that this and all the days to come, may bring only good to you, and we rejoice that you know from experience, that good for you, is inseparably connected with the good you bring to others. But this is not a lecture, only a kind word from an affectionate father to a much loved and only son on the occasion of his 21st birthday.

John D. Rockefeller

Brown University
Providence, R.I.

---

11 Slater Hall
Prov. R.I.
February 3, 1895

Dear Father,

I want again to thank you for the check which you sent me last week and also for the letter which accompanied it.

I am grateful if my life brings happiness to you; it should bring much more than I have made it. But had I done infinitely better than I have in this particular, I should not even then have made anything like an adequate return for all that you have done for me.

I am glad for the confidence which you say my life inspires in you. I feel that I have but too little confidence in myself; but the very fact of you having faith in me will help me to make the most of my life.

Be assured, dear Father that my greatest happiness will ever be to do my utmost for you and Mother, and not only to keep clean, but be a credit to the honorable and noble record which you have made. People talk about sons being better than their fathers, but if I can be half as generous, half as unselfish, and half as kindly affectionate to my fellow men as you have been, I shall not feel that my life has been in vain.

Affectionately,
John

26 Broadway
New York

Providence, R.I.
April 2, 1897

My dear Father:

Dr. Morehouse of the Home Mission Society called me to other day to ask if I would be willing to fill one of the vacancies on the Board of Directors of the Baptist Home Mission Society.

I thanked him for the honor, and said that I certainly did want to become connected with philanthropic and charitable or Christian organizations, and do what I could in those lines as well as in a business line. Furthermore that my first duty as well as my pleasure after this year would be to help you in whatever capacity or position you might see fit. That I therefore felt that my time belonged to you.

If there are other organizations of a similar character to the one mentioned in which I could better represent you and your interests, I should not feel justified in considering this call. If not, and it is your wish and pleasure that I become a member of the Home Mission Board, I shall be glad to comply with their request although I could be of but little use to them until I had had some experience.

Personally I am more interested in City Mission work, but these board meetings only come once a month and would not prevent my taking up other lines of work as well.

You know the different Christian and philanthropic organizations. I want to go into those in which I can do the most good, and be of the greatest service to you. Therefore whatever decision you make will be entirely satisfactory to me.

Mr. Faunce has also written me on this same question.

Affectionately,
John

26 Broadway
New York

Dr. Henry Morehouse directed the Baptist Home Mission Society, founded the American Baptist Education Society, and was influential in the creation of the University of Chicago.

---

26 Broadway
New York
July 7th, 1899

Dear Father:

I have found so many things to be attended to on my return to the office that it has seemed impossible to write you sooner although it has been in my mind each day to do so. I want to tell you again how thoroughly I enjoyed our Western trip and how greatly I appreciated this opportunity of rest and change. The trip necessitated a longer vacation for me than I had thought to take this Summer, but I feel so much benefitted by it and so much better able to take up affairs again, that perhaps it is time saved. I send my heartfelt thanks for this added one of a series of kindnesses too long ever to be counted and such as no other son has ever received from a father. I appreciate the confidence which you have always shown in me more deeply than you may ever know, for I certainly cannot express it. It is my happiness to show it as best I can by my life.

With much love,
John

Forest Hill
Cleveland, Ohio

Junior began working in his father's personal office at 26 Broadway on October 1, 1897. There he joined a staff consisting of F. T. Gates, chief almoner and financial advisor; George D. Rogers, Rockefeller's private secretary; E. V. Cary, bookkeeper and accountant; J. Alva Jenkins, purchasing agent; and Charles O. Heydt, Junior's personal secretary. Junior later said he was given no instructions as to what his duties were but was expected to assume responsibilities as they arose.

In the summer of 1899 Junior went on an extended recreational trip to the far West and Alaska with friends.

Forest Hill
Cleveland, Ohio
July 10th, 1899

Dear John:-

I have your beautiful letter of the 7th. We are so glad you feel better for the vacation and we all hope you will hold the ground gained and be sure to take more rest, and change whenever you think you need it. We all join in thanking you over and over again, for as we review the journey, we are led to appreciate more than we could have expressed to you the plan you adopted, and executed in such a thoroughly satisfactory way.

We receive our pay from you as we go, ten fold. Confidence is a plant of slow growth, but in your case it was a sturdy plant long years ago. We are grateful beyond measure that we can trust, and do trust you in every place without reserve.

Be sure to take good care of your health. This is of the first consideration. All join in love and the hope that some of us will see you soon.

Affectionately,
Father

26 Broadway
New York

---

4 West 54th Street
New York
November 11, 1899

Dear Father,

I want to tell you again of my very deep appreciation of the generous, patient and kindly way in which you have treated me during the anxiety and pressure which has been brought upon you this week largely through me. Most Fathers would have upbraided and stormed, and that too, justly. Because of your forbearance and gentleness you have caused me to feel the more deeply the lesson which this has taught. I would rather have had my right hand cut off than to have caused you this anxiety. My one thought and purpose since I came into the office has been to relieve you in every way possible of the burdens which you have carried so long. To realize now that instead of doing that I have been partially and largely instrumental in adding to your burdens, is bitter and humiliating. My effort has been an honest one although I have failed in its accomplishment. I want fully to acknowledge my mistake and to shoulder the blame which rightfully belongs to me. With your expression of continued confidence which I most truly appreciate, I shall try again in the hope that I can *live* my appreciation of your magnanimity far better than I can express it in words. This has been a hard lesson but it may help me to avoid harder ones in the future.

Affectionately,
John

26 Broadway
New York

In 1936, Junior wrote: "My letter of November 11, 1899 written to Father by me refers to a talk which I had with him at Pocantico Hills one night at which time I told him of the outcome of the leather trading account in which I had engaged and in which, through the treachery of David Lamar commonly known at the 'Wolf of Wall Street' into whose hands I had fallen innocently, I had lost a number of hundred thousands of dollars. After Father was fully informed of the situation, he volunteered to make good the loss."

---

26 Broadway
New York
March 16, 1901

Dear Father:

I enclose a letter recently received from Doctor Muller. It is on the whole most gratifying and of such a nature as to inspire our further confidence in his treatment of Alta. It seems to me, and Parmalee as well, that the only point we need now cover is to get him to state a figure which shall include both the past and future treatment. Otherwise if we go on, on the basis of even $4,000 or $5,000 for what has already been done, the doctor will be inclined to prolong the treatment indefinitely. Since you were so successful in writing the last letter to the doctor perhaps you will be willing to reply to this one.

Captain Bradshaw has purchased the Claflin place in Lakewood for $45,000. Mr. Claflin is already sorry he has made the deal but having received $1,000 on account it cannot be retracted. Mr. H. M. Tilford appears as the purchaser and you are not known. Captain Bradshaw says that he has an agreement with you whereby certain other lots in the rear of the Claflin place are to be sold to you at a fixed price if you so desire. Mr. Claflin has already tried to purchase these lots from Captain Bradshaw, but the Captain replied that an option on them had been given. This matter will hold until your return.

I have your telegram of this morning confirming your former instructions regarding the $250,000 for Y.M.C.A. endowment fund. I am very glad that your are still inclined to do this.

Mr. Bowers writes that the "Cleveland Steel Company" made $11,000 in January and Mr. Higgins believes it will do as well in February. Sales and purchases of slabs are kept neck and neck and we are sold up to and including June on some kinds of material and at a little advance in price for May and June delivery. The mill is running day and night and is doing very well, all things considered.

Affectionately,
John

Forest Hill
Cleveland, Ohio

Rockefeller purchased the Lakewood, New Jersey, property to extend his golfing season. It was the second property purchase outside Cleveland and New York City.

Lamont Bowers was the uncle of F. T. Gates. He joined the Rockefeller organization to manage the Bessemer Steamship Company operating on the Great Lakes. He later assumed other managerial duties including the chief executive position in the Colorado Fuel and Iron Company.

Alta Rockefeller Prentice, John D. Rockefeller's daughter, married E. Parmalee Prentice, a Chicago attorney, on January 17, 1901. Their first home was on West 53rd Street adjoining the rear of Rockefeller's home on West 54th Street. They had three children. In 1901 Alta was being treated for deafness.

26 Broadway
New York
January 13, 1902

Dear Father,

My breath was completely taken away by what you told me regarding my salary for the year that is passed, when I was at the house the other night. I appreciate more deeply than I can tell you this added expression of your love amd confidence.

I cannot feel that any services which I can render are worth to you such a sum as $10,000 a year. Of my ability I have always had a very poor opinion, but I need not assure you that such as it is, it is wholly and absolutely devoted to your interests, and that now and always you can trust me as you always have.

In view of the enlarged home cares and responsibilities which I have assumed in the last year, this increase in income is most acceptable. I can only say thank you again and redouble my efforts to be of service to you and prove my gratitude.

Affectionately,
John

Pocantico Hills, N.Y.

John D. Rockefeller, Jr. married Abby Greene Aldrich on October 1, l901 at Warwick, Rhode Island. They had six children: Abby Rockefeller Mauze, John D. Rockefeller 3rd, Nelson A. Rockefeller, Laurance S. Rockefeller, Winthrop Rockefeller, and David Rockefeller. Their first homes were 13 West 54th Street, New York City and Abeyton Lodge, Pocantico Hills, New York.

Forest Hill
Cleveland, Ohio
July 8, 1905

Dear Son:-

I have yours of the 5th with regard to your house question at Pocantico.

You need not pay for any of the work of the mechanics about the house hereafter. Let the watchman's wages for last winter be charged to the house, as you suggest. The care of the grounds about the house, as well as the flowers, I will pay. If you are entirely satisfied to do so, you may continue to pay half of Tony's wages for the services which he renders to you in the house, as you suggest.

I am so happy that you and Abby enjoy the place. I found my attachment to it increasing with each day of my stay, and it was with great reluctance I left it. Now I am absorbed in dear old Forest Hill, and busy indeed, and more grateful than I can tell you for the good health which I have and which enables me to do two or three times as much work, Mrs. Tuttle says, as I used to do when she was here before. Osteopathy! Osteopathy! Osteopathy!

This is a quiet day, and we are celebrating my sixty-sixth birthday. At five o'clock we expect an Italian band of thirty-five and a very few friends to hear them play. I wish you could both be with us.

We have Edith's baby, and she is a dear.

All unite in love to you and Abby.

Affectionately,
Father

Pocantico Hills, N.Y.

Edith Rockefeller, John D. Rockefeller's daughter, married Harold Fowler McCormick on November 26, 1895. Their daughter, Mathilda McCormick, was born on April 8, 1905. They had three children who lived to maturity: Harold Fowler McCormick, Jr., Muriel McCormick Hubbard, and Mathilda McCormick Oser.

Mrs. Tuttle was the telegrapher who maintained communications between Forest Hill and 26 Broadway.

---

26 Broadway
New York
December 31, 1906

Dear Father:

Not long since you spoke to me of your thought to found a large trust to which you might turn over considerable sums of money to be devoted to philanthropy, education, science and religion. At the time I raised the question as to whether it would be possible to get together a single group of men who could be expected to have knowledge and interest along so many different lines. I desire to make herewith an alternative suggestion, which is the result of frequent conferences with Mr. Gates and Mr. Murphy,

It is, that you establish several trusts, incorporating under existing state or Federal Laws, or securing special charters from the State or the Federal Government if desirable.

Let the Board of Trustees of these various foundations for the present consist in each instance of Mr. Gates, Mr. Murphy and myself as a nucleus, with two added members, and let the incorporation be made with a Board of five. This would make possible early incorporation and the transfer by you to these various trusts of whatever sums you might desire in the immediate future.

Let the question of working out a permanent organization of these Boards be taken up at our leisure, with a view to the selection of the very best men available in each instance. This can not be done in a hurry, but may require several years of thought and study.

In the letter of gift from yourself to each of the respective trusts, let it be stated that during your life you will retain a veto power. This power could be extended to the life of your son if you thought wise, although my present feeling is that such a request would tend to lessen the interest of the Trustees and free them from responsibility. In the remote future you must of necessity trust to the character and integrity of the men who come after you. Is it not reasonable to suppose that those whom you or your family may select will doubtless be quite as trustworthy as those selected in the appointed ways hereafter?

This method of organization has the following advantages:

1. It can be quickly effected, enabling you at an early date to make such gifts to the various trusts as you may desire.
2. It does not require the elaborate working out in advance of the detail of organization and the selection of the Board.
3. The veto power being in your hands makes the situation practically the same as though the funds were being dispensed through your own office as at present, only that their permanent abiding place will have been selected and arranged by yourself.

We suggest the foundation along the lines above outlined of the following trusts, and I will state them in the order of their importance as we see it:

1. ESTABLISHMENT OF A FUND FOR THE PROMOTION OF CHRISTIAN CIVILIZATION;

Through this agency you would contribute the amounts which you are contributing annually through the American Baptist Missionary Society, to the foreign work of the Young Men's Christian Association, and such special gifts as you have made of late years to the Congregational Board of Foreign Missions, the United Presbyterian Board of Foreign Missions, and to Young Men's Christian Association buildings in the foreign field. $500,000 of annual income would probably not more than cover these items. In addition there would lie open not only the foreign missionary fields of all denominations, reached through their respective Boards, but the Y.M.C.A., the educational field, and generally any philanthropic or social work in the foreign field which might be regarded as worthy of assistance. The purpose of this foundation is necessarily so broad that so long as the world stands funds could wisely and usefully be dispensed in accordance therewith.

In addition to the three gentlemen of your office we would

suggest for Trustees of this fund, Mr. John R. Mott, of the International Young Men's Christian Association, who has perhaps a broader knowledge of missions and Christian work throughout the world than any other living man, and he might some day become the secretary of the Board, giving his entire time to the work: Mr. Robert E. Speer, secretary of the Presbyterian Board of Foreign Missions, a man second only to Mr. Mott in ability, education, breadth of view, and sympathy. It would be desirable to select the other members with the greatest care and without any sense of haste.

We feel that a contribution of $25,000,000 could be made to this Board at the outset. As I have already pointed out the income of half that amount would be required to meet the contributions which you are already making.

2. ESTABLISHMENT OF A FUND FOR THE PROMOTION OF CHRISTIAN CIVILIZATION IN THE UNITED STATES.

This would be similar to the Fund for the Foreign Fields. The income from this fund could meet the contributions to the Home Mission Society which you are now making, those to the City Mission Society, and those to the various State Conventions; also all Contributions to churches might be met from this fund; contributions to Y.M.C.A.s in this country, as well as gifts for other forms of social and philanthropic work. The income from a gift of $5,000,000 to this trust would probably not much more than meet the contributions which you are now making to the objects above referred to, and $10,000,000 might perhaps be safely given.

As to the Trustees of this foundation we are not at present prepared to make any suggestion beyond the three gentlemen in the office.

3. A TRUST TO HOLD FUNDS WHICH WILL EVENTUALLY BE REQUIRED FOR THE UNIVERSITY OF CHICAGO, THE GENERAL EDUCATION BOARD AND THE ROCKEFELLER INSTITUTE FOR MEDICAL RESEARCH.

The University will require as much as $10,000,000 more, the General Education Board an equal amount, and the Rockefeller Institute probably not less than $5,000,000. We therefore suggest that this foundation be one of $ 25,000,000.

Unlike the other foundations this would not require to be a permanent foundation, but in the letter of gift it could be stated that within a period of say twenty-five years not only the income but the principal of the fund should be distributed in the ratio above suggested to the three institutions for whom it would be founded.

As Trustees of this fund, in addition to the three gentlemen in the office, I have thought of Harold and Parmalee, or perhaps instead of Parmalee, Mr. Ryerson of Chicago. Mr. Ryerson would be a splendid man for the position, the only question being whether his relationship to the University of Chicago would incapacitate him. We feel that no one of these institutions in whose interest this fund is to be created should know of its establishment, hence the desirability of keeping the Board small and in a sense in the family,

This, then, gives you the lines along which we are thinking. If to any extent whatever these thoughts meet with your approval we will be glad to give them further study with a view to maturing something definite and tangible.

Affectionately
John

4 West 54th Street
New York

Starr J. Murphy joined the office staff in 1901 as the in-house legal advisor. He conducted many investigations of potential beneficiaries of the Rockefeller largesse.

The General Education Board was chartered by Congress in 1903. It sought to aid education at all levels throughout the United States but with an emphasis on black education in the South. It made its last appropriation in 1964.

The Rockefeller Institute for Medical Research was founded in 1901. The first institution in the United States devoted solely to biomedical research, it is now The Rockefeller University.

New York
January 15, 1907

Dear Son:

I have just read yours of December 31st, with reference to the establishment of trusts for different purposes.

I will continue to study these suggestions, but I think it safe for you to move, with the thought that something will be wrought out along these lines.

Affectionately,
Father

26 Broadway
New York

Forest Hill
Cleveland, Ohio
September 18, 1907

Dear Son:

Please have five hundred (500) shares of Standard Oil stock transferred to Edith, and five hundred (500) shares to Alta, and when the transfers are made, have them both notified. And while you are about it, you might as well have five hundred (500) shares transferred to yourself, and notify me of the whole job lot.

Affectionately,
Father

26 Broadway
New York

P.S. Of course, I would not be giving any of you this, only that it seems as though the stock would not be worth anything and

I want full credit for the desire to help out. However, please do not let any of it get out of your hands without seeing me.

Forest Hill
Cleveland, Ohio
July 27, 1908

Dear Son:-

In the absence of Henry Cooper from the office, I required information regarding the D.& R. G. notes and the contract, but could not get it until his return.

Please arrange so that any important matter of this kind can be reviewed in the office, in the absence of the particular individual having it specially in hand.

Affectionately,
Father

26 Broadway
New York

Henry E. Cooper was a friend of Junior's at Brown. He was a member of the office staff from 1907 to 1912 and was the chairman of the committee on investments.

Rockefeller had a large investment in the Denver and Rio Grande Railroad bonds.

---

26 Broadway
New York
July 30, 1908

Dear Father:

Your letter of July 27 with reference to your inquiry regarding D. & R. G. notes and contract, and your inability to get the information which you desired in Mr. Cooper's absence, was received.

Mr. Cary, to whom Mr. Lovatt went for information in the matter, turned to the contract in the files. The information desired was not in the contract and was such as could be had only by application to the syndicate managers, with whom the date of calling payments is optional. Mr. Cary called up Mr. Marston's office to procure this, but Mr. Marston was out of town. I do not know what more he could have done.

All purchases and sales, or contracts which are made by any of us in the office are reported to Mr. Cary, who has access to the data pertaining thereto and who if the query is possible of answer could probably give you the answer desired. I think our system is adequate.

Affectionately,
John

Forest Hill
Cleveland, Ohio

Hotel Bon Air
Augusta, Georgia
January 18, 1909

Dear Son:-

I thank you a thousand times for the fur coat and cap and mittens. I did not feel that I could afford such luxuries, and am grateful for a son who is able to buy them for me. Be assured they are much appreciated. Mother unites with me in thanking you.

Affectionately,
Father

26 Broadway
New York

---

26 Broadway
New York
January 29, 1909

Dear Father:

I am in receipt of a birthday check which comes with a regularity and promptness that is deeply appreciated by me as it is thoughtful of you. Many, many thanks for the gift and the affectionate remembrance which it indicates.

As I said to you the other day I feel that I do not begin to express my thanks and gratitude to you for the many generous and thoughtful, delightful things which you are constantly doing for me and my family. You are supplying a house for us in the city, which is so comfortable, so attractive and so dear to us. Then, too there is the country home which we have the use of through your generosity and of which we are also fond. In addition there is the enjoyment of the Pocantico Place and the opportunity to participate with you in its management and development, which is so great a delight and recreation to both Abby and me. Your willingness to share with us this pleasure and privilege is as unusual as it is gratifying to us. The use of the horses, summer and winter, is such a tremendous convenience and delight to us all. What it means to us we could hardly realize unless deprived of it.

In addition you give us children the yearly allowance, besides the generous Christmas and birthday gifts, and in these latter the "in-laws" are permitted to share on equal terms with your own children.

But even this list does not do more that outline the many gifts which you have given us. I am increasingly sensible of your generosity in connection with the very large and valuable real estate holdings which you have turned over to me in the last couple of years. Over and above all of these material gifts there are those things of far greater,—yes, inestimable value,—the constant personal indications of your love and confidence and affection of which you are such a lavish giver.

When I try, although so weakly, to express my appreciation of all these things to you, I mean to include Mother as well, for are not you and Mother one?

So you see, as I reflect upon my blessings on this birthday, I find, as I constantly do when I take inventory, that my cup is always more than running over and my heart goes up in a prayer of thanksgiving to the Heavenly Father for His great and wonderful goodness to me, typified on earth by the generosity and love of such an earthly father and mother as no other son has ever known.

That God will give me strength to be equal to the task to which He has called me, and to be worthy of the love and confidence which my dear ones have reposed in me, is my daily prayer.

With deepest thanks and love to you and Mother, I am,

Affectionately,
John

Hotel Bon Air
Augusta, Ga.

John D. Rockefeller established his country home in Pocantico Hills, Tarrytown, New York in 1896 when he purchased a large house called Kykuit on a hill overlooking the Hudson River. He gradually added to his first purchase and by 1937 owned over 3,500 acres of land. The original house burned down in 1904 and was replaced by a stone mansion. He initially built a four-hole golf course, later rebuilt as a reversible nine-hole course providing a full 18 holes.

John D. Rockefeller, Jr.'s family spent weekends in a second large house on the estate. It was purchased in 1904 and extensively remodeled. This house was torn down in 1937 when Junior and his wife moved into Kykuit after Rockefeller Senior died.

---

26 Broadway
New York
February 1, 1909

Dear Father:

I have just been going over a comparative statement of my accounts for the years since my marriage. Since you expressed interest in my total expenditures a year or so ago I am thinking that you may be interested to glance at this account, copy of which I enclose herewith.

I am quite aghast at the large increase in my total expenditures last year. The increase is, in round numbers, $19,000. It is accounted for in half a dozen items:

The summer expense item has hitherto been charged to my personal account. There is therefore in the sum of these two an increase over last year of $3,000 partly due to the higher cost of a house, etc., in Bar Harbor, partly to a present which I made to Abby.

In the donation account there is an increase of $9,000. This is a great surprise to me, but the money has all gone into good places. The total is considerably more that I had planned to give.

An increase of $1,000 in maintenance, which means, ice, coal, electric light, and things of that sort.

An increase of $2,000 in food, partly due to our larger family, and partly to the increase in the cost of food.

An increase of $2,000 in wages. We have now two trained nurses constantly in our employ at $100 a month each. We have added a housekeeper this last year at $50 a month. There was in addition a special trained nurse during Abby's illness last summer. We also keep the Tarrytown house open the year round and have beside two servants in the house a colored man and the watchman on the payroll.

This covers a large part of the increase.

Personal Account covers all traveling expenses, my gifts to Abby, my own clothes, and things not chargeable to other accounts.

Incidentals covers presents made, things bought for ourselves, such as books, objects of art, doctors' bills (which last summer ran up to about $2,000), etc.

Affectionately,
John

Hotel Bon Air
Augusta, Ga

After several summers of renting cottages along the Massachusetts shore, Junior rented Sears Cottage in Bar Harbor, Maine, for the summer of 1908. His son Nelson Aldrich Rockefeller was born there. In 1910 he bought a house, the Eyrie, in Seal Harbor, Maine. After 1910 the family spent part of most summers in Seal Harbor. The house was demolished in 1961.

Junior's total expenditures for 1908 were $65,918.47.

Hotel Bon Air
Augusta, Georgia
February 2, 1909

Dear Son:-

We deeply appreciate your beautiful letter of the 29th, and are so thankful for you and Abby and the dear children and are so much comforted and sustained to know what you are and all that you may be to us and to others in the time to come. We lean upon you more and more, and be assured we are more appreciative than we have yet expressed or even undertaken to express in words of your thoughtful kindness and constant attention to all that ministers to our well being and happiness.

There is and will be much for you all to do in the world, and it is a matter of the greatest concern to us that you may be better and better fitted for these peculiar responsibilities, for which you have thus far shown yourselves so eminently qualified.

All goes well with us, and we unite in love.

Affectionately,
Father

26 Broadway
New York

---

26 Broadway
New York
March 17, 1909

Dear Father,

Your two letters of March 15th are received. The one giving me the remainder of the splendid tract of land of which the Rockefeller Institute has bought a portion, the other giving me your Linseed holdings, and all of this in addition to the Buffalo property which you so recently gave me. The monetary value of these gifts is of course tremendous, running into a number of millions of dollars and I do not for a moment under estimate its proportions. But to me their greatest worth lies in the fact that they give evidence of your deep confidence in me and in my earnest purpose under God to use my life and my opportunities and my possessions as my Heavenly Father may direct and my earthly parents would approve. This confidence I prize above all else, and to merit such approval do I daily strive.

Dear Father, I thank you most truly. A deep feeling of solemnity, of responsibility, almost of awe, comes over me as I contemplate these gifts, and my heart rises in silent prayer to God that he will teach me to be a good and faithful steward as my Father has been, that I may each day be more of a help and comfort to my dear parents who have all their lives spent themselves so lavishly for their children.

With truest affection,

John

Forest Hill
Cleveland, Ohio

---

26 Broadway
New York
March 19, 1909

Dear Father:

Referring to your proposed gifts to me of property remaining in the tract from which you have given certain portions to the Rockefeller Institute, and the Linseed stock, there arise in connection with these two gifts a number of questions which must be taken up and disposed of. I am sure you will allow me to discuss these questions with you in an absolutely impersonal way as though these gifts were being made to some other member of the family, and that I am sure you will not construe my attitude as indicating a lack of appreciation or of deepest gratitude. When you expressed your desire to give the Riverside property to Edith and learned what it would cost to carry the property you yourself said that some way should be devised so that the property might not be a burden to Edith. What I shall say in this letter or in subsequent letters, therefore, I am sure you will accept in the spirit in which it is said.

First: As to the property adjacent to the Rockefeller Institute, I assume that you have given this property to me largely as a further generous expression of your confidence in and affection for me, partly because it is your desire, although inferred by me rather than expressed by you, that this property should be held by your heirs for the further requirements of the Rockefeller Institute or other kindred philanthropic institutions which may be developed and require land as the years go by. I do not assume, until this latter purpose has been served to its fullest extent, which would be some years hence, that you had thought of it as a gift which would bring in revenue or be convertible into cash. The taxes on the property which you still own amounted this past year to about $9,000.

If I am right in the assumption just set forth would it be your wish to pay the taxes in the future as in the past, although the property might stand in my name?

Again, I wrote you a short time ago that the institute with our consent was now making an effort to have 65th Street, which is owned by the City but has never been cut through, permanently closed. If this effort is successful, as it undoubtedly will be, the institute would then desire to buy from the city with funds which we will ask you to supply, the portion of the Street contiguous to its property, and it has been our thought that you, as the owner of the balance of the property, would, in your own interest, desire to buy the remainder of 65th Street where it crosses your property. This total purchase on behalf of the institute as well as yourself, may run as high as $50,000 or $60,000, of which you would own and hold from two-thirds to three-fourths of the land thus bought. Obviously, were I the owner of the property I could hardly make this investment, and yet, in the interest of the property, it should be made.

Again, I wrote you the other day that Mr. Murphy was preparing a paper as a result of our mutual deliberation which, when signed by you would give the Institute the right to buy at the same price which any other purchaser might be willing to pay a strip of seventy-five feet in width and running the length of the new hospital building on the west, in order to permanently assure to the hospital adequate light and air. In view of the proposed transfer of this property from you to me, I have talked with Mr. Murphy today regarding the advisability of your selling outright to the Institute at this time this 75 ft. strip instead of signing such an agreement as above proposed. I am inclined to favor this idea for it would permanently dispose of the question of adequate protection for the hospital and not leave it to be taken up after your death and possibly after mine when there might be complications because of minor heirs and the end which you would desire to have accomplished might either be delayed or frustrated. If this sale were now made to the institute it would reduce by that much your holdings and reduce proportionately the taxes to be borne by either you or me hereafter on the remaining property.

These matters I present for your consideration as they are receiving ours, and until some decision has been reached regarding them it has seemed to me simpler to delay the execution of a deed.

As to the Linseed Company, your desire to turn over this stock to me can be legally effected by the simple turning over the securities to me and their removal from your vaults to mine. The certificates of stock are in the name of Mr. Lovatt and various brokers' clerks, none in your name, hence no transfer of stock is necessary. Mr. Murphy suggests that you write a letter to Mr. Cary instructing him to give to me these certificates of stock. I will then have them deposited in my safe deposit vault and the gift will thus be completed. It might also be well for you to write me a letter stating that you had so instructed Mr. Cary in line with the wish expressed in your letter of March 15th to give me your interest in this company.

Since you took over the Linseed Company you have been providing it current working capital on an open book account, neither receiving security for the moneys advanced nor even the notes of the Linseed Company. A receipt for the money paid from time to time is all the evidence of the debt which you hold. So long as you retain the control of the company your claim was substantially and practically safe, although Mr. Murphy and I have agreed that a better method will be the actual passing of notes when each advance is made and the endorsement on the back of these notes of payments when these sums are returned to you, even if the question of interest were by a written agreement left to be adjusted monthly or quarterly at a rate to be currently agreed upon. The moment, however, that the control of the company passes from your hands, while you have practically the same assurance that your advances will be refunded, in case of your death there might be material difficulty in proving your legal claim to the moneys advanced.

But if you do not finance the company, of course I cannot, and if the company were able to float bonds in order to provide money for its requirements this would only be possible at such a high rate of interest as would fix upon the company a current charge which its present earnings would hardly bear.

In a previous letter you very kindly said that in connection with the proposed gift to me of this stock that you would continue your interest in the management of the company as heretofore. Was it your intention to imply that you would finance the company as heretofore, or if it was not at that time, would you be willing to do so from year to year?

We will in any event work out some plan whereby your advances shall be better protected than they have been in the past.

Mr. Murphy, Mr. Cooper and I have talked not a little about Linseed matters in the past few days. The capitalization of the company is $32,000,000. Mr. Cooper says that the last appraisal of the plants of the company was something under $5,000,000. I presume that the present producing capacity of the company could be duplicated easily for $5,000,000, but assuming the assets of the company to be worth $5,000,000 the company has earned during the past five years, in addition to the interest on its working capital, say $200,000 a year, but nothing has been charged to depreciation of plants and these surplus earnings have been all too little in amounts to put back into the plants in betterments, etc. It is evident then that, regardless of the capitalization of the company on anything like the present basis of earnings it can never hope to do more than keep its head above water. To do otherwise means a reduction in cost of manufacture and the sales of its product, or a larger profit in the astute forecasting of crop conditions and seed purchases.

I believe that there can and should be economies made in the manufacture and sale of oil, and with accumulated experience there may be some increase of profit in seed buying. In any event it is our purpose to go into the entire matter with a fine tooth comb with a view to ascertaining in each department whether the best possible results are being attained and if not how they can be attained.

I am not at this moment able to make any suggestions nor draw any conclusions. I have put down in this letter my thoughts of the last few days that the matters when presented will be in your mind as well.

Affectionately
John

Forest Hill
Cleveland, Ohio

Rockefeller gave Junior his entire holding in American Linseed consisting of 88,400 shares of common stock and 101,800 shares of preferred. In thanking his father for the gift Junior reported that the net worth of the company was $6,400,000, making the preferred stock worth $40 per share.

---

26 Broadway
New York
January 11, 1910

Dear Father;

Since you have upon previous occasions expressed an interest in the total amount of money which I spend in a year you will be interested to know that my total expenditures for the year 1909 is $86,288.35. Subtracting from this amount $25,000 which I gave to Brown, leaves a total of $58,238.35. The total last year was $65,918.47. This excess in 1908 is accounted for by the amount which I gave away during that year as compared with the amount given away in 1909 less the $25,000 above referred to.

Affectionately,
John

Hotel Bon Air
Augusta, Ga.

---

26 Broadway
New York
January 12th 1911

Dear Father:

In making your gift of $32,000,000 to the General Educational Board you set aside two-thirds of that amount, or approximately $22,000,000 having in mind the future needs of the University and of the Rockefeller Institute. After having set aside the $10,000,000 recently pledged to the University of Chicago there remains of the principal in the fund about $2,500,000. Mr. Gates, Mr. Murphy and I are now suggesting that you direct the General Education Board to turn over to the Trustees of the Rockefeller Institute for Medical Research when and as the trustees may make requisition therefore, $2,000,000 for the further endowment of the institute. A letter to the General Education Board giving these directions I am enclosing for your signature if it meets with your approval.

The purpose of making this final disposition of an added $2,000,000 of the fund at this time is in order to free just that amount of money from the liability for taxation under the new inheritance tax law for as the matter now stands your having the right to change the designation of the balance of the two-thirds of the $32,000,000, this balance would be subject to taxation.

The Institute will probably need an additional $1,000,000 of endowment at the beginning of the next fiscal year, July 1st, in order to carry on the work as at present organized. Within the next couple years the facilities now afforded in the Institute building and in the Hospital, if used to their fullest extent, will probably require the income of still another million. There is no question as to the proper and useful employment of $2,000,000 more of money in the institute work.

You will note that the letter to the General Education Board directs that the $2,000,000 be set aside now and turned over to the Trustees of the Institute when and as called for by the Trustees. The Trustees at present are five in number, Mr. Gates, and Mr. Murphy and I being three, so that we would be in the majority and could ask for the funds as soon as we thought it wise, or delay indefinitely calling for payment if that seemed better. This seems to be a perfectly safe and at the same time flexible way of providing that this $2,000,000 shall finally go to the Institute without stating at this time the date of payment.

We are not enclosing a list of securities. It has not been prepared, but will be if this letter meets with your approval and is signed.

Affectionately,
John

Hotel Bon Air
Augusta, Ga

---

26 Broadway
New York
February 24, 1911

Dear Father:

We have been discussing in the office of late the wisdom of your making investments in Bank and Trust Company stocks as satisfactory opportunities present. Aside from the fact that such investments, if properly selected, ought to be safe, as regards trust companies they ought to lead to your having opportunities to participate in large pieces of financing which such companies handle.

There is an opportunity now to purchase 3500 shares of Equitable Trust Company stock at 500. The stock paid 24% last year, earns a little more, and is expected to advance.

One hundred shares of Mercantile Trust Company stock have been offered at 750. The yield is about 4% but the earnings 8%.

Both of these companies are now controlled by the Equitable Life Assurance Company which latter is obliged to sell out its stock holdings by reason of late insurance laws.

If this general policy of investment appeals to you we will look into the matter further and make specific recommendations. We favor it.

Affectionately,
John

Hotel Bon Air
Augusta, Ga.

The Hotel Bon Air
Augusta, Georgia
March 13th, 1911

Dear Son:-

Answering yours of March 8th with reference to the purchase of the stock of the Equitable Trust Company. I incline to buy 6,000 shares. If you and Mr. Gates object please telegraph; if you do not object, insist on having 6,000 shares. In these matters we must have some assurance.

Affectionately,
Father

26 Broadway
New York

---

26 Broadway
New York
March 17, 1911

Dear Father:

I have had a conference this afternoon with Mr. Krech, President of the Equitable Trust Company. I find that Kuhn, Loeb & Co. have altogether 4365 shares of Equitable Trust Co. stock, for which they paid $500 a share. This stock is only a portion of it held in the firm name, the balance appearing in the name of clerks. In view of your willingness to take more than 4,500 shares, and since it is not necessary that your entire holdings should stand in your own name I have agreed with Mr. Krech that you would take 5,000 shares, 3,000 in your own name the balance to be split up in the names of several of the men in the office.

I have also agreed that after the balance of the 14,000 shares now offered for sale has been disposed of, if it should seem desirable to place a few hundred shares more in order to secure business you would be willing to consider giving up 500 shares of the present purchase. This is optional with you.

Mr. Krech would be glad to have you have a representative on the Board and on the Executive Committee. The latter meets once a week. He is hoping that this investment on your part will lead you to turn what business you can to the company, and on the other hand it will be the aim of the company, whenever participations are offered to it, to give you an opportunity to share in such participations if you so desire. I think it would be well for you to have a representative on the Board and probably on the executive committee. Mr. Gates will perhaps be burdened enough with the Missouri Pacific. It might be well to put Mr. Cooper in. What is your wish in the matter?

Affectionately,
John

Golf House
Lakewood, N.J.

Golf House
Lakewood, N.J.
March 20th, 1911

Dear Son:-

Answering yours of March 17th, I hardly think we will want to sell out the 500 shares of Equitable Trust Co. stock but we can see if the question is called.

I may be wrong but I still incline to think it might be well to have 500 or 1,000 shares more.

If you think best you may have Mr. Cooper placed on the Board and on the Executive Committee. I know of no reason why we should not throw business in the way of this Company.

Affectionately,
Father

26 Broadway
New York

---

26 Broadway
New York
April 25, 1911

Dear Father:

I talked at some length with Senator Aldrich regarding the Rockefeller Foundation bill. He talked with Senator Gallinger, who had previously introduced the bill, and they both agreed with us that it is best not to re-introduce the bill, until the Standard Oil decision is handed down. I told Mr. Aldrich of our conference with the President on the matter through Mr. Gates and of the Attorney-General's attitude, and suggested that he mention the matter to the President himself. This he did. The President said he thought the charter ought to be granted but agreed that it would be better not to re-introduce the bill until after the Standard Oil decision.

Mr. Aldrich has talked with a number of different people from time to time regarding the decision and seems to be of the opinion that very possibly no decision will be handed down until just before the adjournment of the Supreme Court late in May. He was disposed to believe that the decision will be adverse to the company, but thinks the Court will clearly define the law and hopes that it will point out a legal way for the conduct of large corporations.

Twice when walking in the streets I met Mr. Hughes and both times had a talk with him on general subjects. He inquired pleasantly after Mother and you.

I thank you for the clippings regarding Doctor Aked which you have sent me of late.

Affectionately,
John

Golf House
Lakewood, N.J.

The bill introduced by Senator Gallinger provided for a Federal charter for the proposed Rockefeller Foundation. Senator Nelson W. Aldrich, 1841–1915, Senator from Rhode Island, was the father of Abby Aldrich Rockefeller. Senator Jacob H. Gallinger of New Hampshire served in the U.S. Senate from 1891 to 1918. He was born in 1837 and died in l918.

The Standard Oil decision by the Supreme Court ordered the dissolution of the Standard Oil Company, New Jersey, successor to the Standard Oil Trust, into 32 separate companies.

Charles Evans Hughes, a New York attorney, was active in the Fifth Avenue Baptist Church with Junior. He was the Republican candidate for president in 1914. Later he was chief justice of the Supreme Court. The president was William Howard Taft.

26 Broadway
New York
November 13, 1911

Dear Father:

Answering your letter of November 11th, if Mr. Greene were to undertake to secure the passage through Congress of the Rockefeller Foundation charter, the expense would simply be his own personal expenses and what small amount you might think it best to pay him, probably a few hundred dollars.

You ask "Why not consider getting a charter in the State of New York or some of the other States." This is a matter which we carefully considered before applying to Congress. Since the scope of the foundation is so broad, not only national but worldwide, and since the amount which it was assumed you would eventually be disposed to give to the foundation was so unprecedented, it seemed as though its care and distribution should be in the hands of the representatives of the people at large rather than the representatives of any State. Again, whatever body grants such a charter would have the right at its own pleasure to change the conditions or terms of the charter. It is possible that a State, desirous of controlling a fund so large and so potent, might in time insist that the Board of Directors should be made up of people residing in that State alone. It would also have the right to direct that all of the income of the fund be used within the boundaries of the State. That such action would be taken by a State is not probable but it is possible.

I has seemed to us that a national charter, if obtainable, would be the safest and broadest. We have recognized from the first that if that could not be secured a State charter would be the next best thing. As you doubtless know many States have volunteered to incorporate such a foundation.

This morning I called upon Senator Root to ask him for letters of introduction for Mr. Abraham Flexner, who is going abroad for our small committee. I took the opportunity of asking Senator Root what his judgement would be with reference to having some paid representative father the bill in Washington. He said he feared that while perfectly legitimate any kind of lobbying would be misconstrued and used against the measure. I will advise with Senator Aldrich when the first opportunity is presented. In the meantime we will do nothing.

Affectionately
John

Forest Hill
Cleveland, Ohio

Jerome Greene was secretary of the Rockefeller Institute for Medical Research and a Rockefeller office associate.

Abraham Flexner was secretary of the General Education Board. His brother Simon Flexner was the director of the Rockefeller Institute for Medical Research. The efforts to obtain a federal charter were unsuccessful.

The Rockefeller Foundation was chartered in the state of New York in 1913. Senator Elihu Root of New York served in the U.S. Senate from 1909 to 1915. He was born in 1845 and died in 1937.

---

26 Broadway
New York
May 19, 1913

Dear Father:-

Mr. Murphy and Mr. Greene are both hoping that you may feel disposed to attend the first meeting of the Rockefeller Foundation, which is to be held in the office here on Thursday of this week at twelve o'clock. The other incorporators, including Dr. Judson of Chicago, Dr. Rose of the Hookworm Commission, also Dr. Flexner and Mr. Gates, with those of us here, will all be present. How much we should enjoy having the founder of the fund at this meeting for organization goes without saying. I told the gentlemen, however, that I would not think of urging you to come, nor did I believe you would feel that you cared to do so.

This note is simply to tell you how welcome you would be if you should feel disposed to attend the meeting.

Affectionately,
John

Pocantico Hills, N.Y.

---

26 Broadway
New York
March 26, 1914

Dear Father:-

I have told Mother that I would thank you for the letter from Charlie Adams and your reply, which you sent her to read. She was much interested in both. Your letter is a beautiful one. I am venturing to keep the copy myself. Mother also was glad to see the sprig from the camphor plant which Mr. Sims sent her at your request and sends her thanks.

I have been going to Pocantico Wednesday and Saturday for the last couple of weeks, since it leaves a shorter time between visits. With Mother's entire consent, as the result of a talk with Dr. Flexner about her condition, also with Dr. Allen's full concurrence, Dr. Janeway, one of the Directors of the Institute, and one of the ablest diagnosticians in the city, went up with Dr. Allen to see Mother on Sunday. He practically confirms Dr. Allen's diagnosis. Mother is much interested in doing whatever the Doctors think will conduce to her improvement. She has talked of going to a sanitarium. This has given us an opportunity to introduce a very strict regime, which diverts her and at the same time will be most helpful. The coughing has weakened her somewhat, but that is much better now and she is getting good rest at night. The Doctor is planning to get her out on the piazza within a couple of days. An invalid's couch on wheels, with an awning over it, is being purchased, also all sorts of wraps, so that she can be taken out without being dressed and with the least possible discomfort. She is looking forward to the change.

Both she and I have been glad that you have not been at Pocantico these last weeks, for the weather has been so unpleasant you could not have been out at all. The great quantities of snow have made walking and driving almost impossible, for frequent thaws between storms have spoiled both the sleighing and driving. The snow is going rapidly now, however, and in another week or two the roads ought to be good. Mother misses you, but is glad to feel that you are having a good rest, and while she will welcome you home, realizes that you should have this change.

Affectionately,
John

Golf House
Lakewood, N.J.

Laura Spelman Rockefeller died at Pocantico Hills on April 12, 1915.

---

26 Broadway
New York
April 3, 1914

Dear Father:

I quote the following from a letter from Mr. Greene, which I know will interest you:

> We are having the time of our lives down here, thanks to your father's unfailing attention to our comfort and pleasure. I spend every morning on the links with him and the latter part of every afternoon motoring. Such a good vacation I think I never have had. The opportunity of getting to know your father better was one to which I had been looking forward, but I had not anticipated seeing so much of him or enjoying so constantly his thoughtful kindness. Except for an

occasional word on the links, we have not talked business, but his observations on men and affairs generally have been most interesting.

Mr. Murphy has spoken most enthusiastically of his delightful stay with you.

The Committee of the House on Mines and Mining has asked me to appear before it to give information regarding the miners' strike in Colorado. The Committee which went to Colorado to investigate the strike, and before which Mr. Welborn appeared for weeks and Mr. Bowers when called, is a Sub-committee of the Committee on Mines and Mining. I have replied that I would be in Washington on Monday next in answer to the invitation. Mr. Murphy will go with me. What possible value any knowledge which I may be able to impart may be to this inquiry, I do not know. However, since the invitation has been extended, I felt it wise to accept it without hesitation.

I am expecting to be at Pocantico tomorrow to see Mother, but as I telegraphed you, shall be returning to New York just as you are coming up, so that, much to my regret, I shall neither be able to meet you on your arrival in New York nor to see you at Pocantico. Next week we are hoping to go to Pocantico for three or four days including the following Sunday, and will then have a good visit.

Affectionately,
John

Golf House
Lakewood, N.J.

J. F. Welborn was made president of the Colorado Fuel and Iron Company in 1907 after Rockefeller obtained a controlling interest in the Company. Lamont M. Bowers was the chairman of the board. Together they maintained a strict control over the affairs of the company and its subsidiaries.

Golf House
Lakewood, N.J.
April 13, 1914

Dear Son:-

I am directing Mr. Cary to give you Ten Thousand (10,000) shares of Colorado Fuel Company stock. In case you are buying or selling this stock, I suggest it would be desirable to keep me posted on what you are doing so that we may not be in conflict.

I feel that you made a splendid effort at Washington before the Committee, and I want you to have an active interest personally in the property. I hope we can make it worth more money.

Affectionately.
Father

26 Broadway
New York

Junior called the events surrounding the coal miners strike in 30 Colorado companies, including the Colorado Fuel and Iron Company, one of the most significant things to ever happen to the Rockefeller family. He appeared twice before congressional committees, and sought viable answers to the struggle between capital and labor in the United States. His life was threatened. He chose as his mentor William Lyon McKenzie King, later prime minister of Canada, and with him developed a plan for industrial representation.

The history of the labor unrest and its local resolution are detailed in the Nevins biographies of Rockefeller Senior and the Fosdick biography of Junior. A different prospective on the events is given in George S. McGovern and Leonard F. Gutteridge, The Great Coalfield War *(Boston: Houghton Mifflin, 1972).*

26 Broadway
New York
August 22, 1914

Dear Father:

On Sunday last, at Warwick, I was present in the morning at a conference on Mr. Morgan's yacht attended by Mr. Morgan, Mr. Davidson, Senator Aldrich, Senator Lippet, who took Mr. Aldrich's place in Washington and Mr. Walters, who is so largely interested in southern railways. This conference was continued during the afternoon at Mr. Aldrich's house. The prevailing opinion was one of discouragement. The New York men felt that with the recent decision in the freight rate case the railroads of the country were generally facing bankruptcy, particularly those who had short term obligations soon to be taken care of. They felt it would be most difficult to secure new capital for the very urgently needed railroad extensions in this country. Furthermore, the opinion prevailed that if the present plan of President Wilson to force through his anti-trust legislation (which there seems no hope of blocking) is carried out other lines of business will be bound and gagged much as the railroads are. Such action would destroy all initiative on the part of capitalists, which never more greatly needed encouragement than at this time when the commerce and the finances of the country are suffering such a check as a result of the European war. The impression made upon me by the conference was that it is the part of wisdom to accumulate cash at present rather than to be tempted into buying bargains and furthermore that for the present at least, railway securities are going to be much less attractive and promising for an investment than formerly. I am wondering whether municipal and Government bonds and bank and trust companies stocks may not prove a safer form of investment for the present at least.

Affectionately,
John

Pocantico Hills, N.Y.

J. P. Morgan was chairman of the board of J. P. Morgan & Co. His father, the elder J. P. Morgan, died in 1913. Henry P. Davison was a Morgan partner. Henry Walters was chairman of the board and general manager of the Atlantic Coastline and the Louisville and Nashville railroads. Henry Frederick Lippit of Rhode Island served in the U.S. Senate from 1911 to 1917.

Junior misspelled the names of Davidson and Lippit.

Pocantico Hills,
New York
January 28, 1915

Dear Son:

I am giving you Forty thousand (40,000) shares of the common stock of the Colorado Fuel and Iron Company, with the hope that we may make it much more valuable than it is today.

I take the greatest satisfaction in the way you bore yourself through all the long and tedious examinations of this week, from Monday morning until Wednesday night, before the Industrial Commission. I believe great good will come out of it. Mother and I are very proud, and more than satisfied with the result. I do not think of anyone who could have done better, nor have I anyone in mind who could have done so well, and I believe that a multitude of people, friends and foes alike, will share this view.

Affectionately,
Father

26 Broadway,
New York

Junior had appeared before the Industrial Relations Commisssion which had been established by Congress in 1912. His testimony reflected his changing views of labor relations because of the Colorado strikes, the Ludlow massacre, and the influence of William Lyon McKenzie King.

Ormond Beach, Florida
February 4, 1915

Dear Son:

I am directing Mr Cary to give you forty thousand (40,000) shares additional of the Colorado Fuel and Iron Company, which please accept with my deep gratitude and bountiful affection.

Affectionately,
Father

26 Broadway
New York

Pocantico Hills, N.Y.
February 7, 1915

Dear Father:-

Nothing has ever touched me more deeply than this last wonderful gift of yours. Coming as it does on top of a similar gift made hardly a week ago, it is the more overwhelming. I fully realize that it is not because of anything I am or have done, but rather the overflowing of your own wonderfully generous and loving nature. And so I accept the gift in a spirit of profound humility and soberness, fully alive to the responsibility for its wise use which is involved, and deeply sensible of your confidence in me which it implies. This confidence I value beyond everything. Dear father, I thank you.

Affectionately
John

Ormond Beach, Florida

---

26 Broadway
New York
September 15, 1915

Dear Father:-

Our conferences last week with Mr. Welborn, Mr. King and Mr. Hicks were most satisfactory. Mr. Welborn and Mr. Hicks started West at the end of the week, and Mr. King left this Monday for Colorado. On Saturday last, Mr. King, Mr. Murphy and I had a four hour conference with Mr. White, the President of the United Mine Workers of America, and Mr. Green, the Secretary-Treasurer. I think you know that last spring Mr. White asked if he might see me. I was either going away or otherwise engaged, and arranged for Mr. Murphy and Mr. Lee to see Mr. White. They had a pleasant interview, of no special significance, and Mr. White expressed the hope that later on he might meet me. On my return from my vacation, Mr. Lee wrote Mr. White that I would be glad to meet him, and the meeting was thus arranged. Mr. White brought with him Mr. Green, his Secretary-Treasurer, without advising us in advance. We found both men intelligent, fair minded and quite without any apparent feeling of hostility. Our conference was understood to be entirely informal and unofficial, simply that of half a dozen men equally interested in a great world problem. We took occasion to make clear to these gentlemen our views in regard to the organization of labor, and read to them the statement which I made before the Industrial Relations Commission in New York last January. While they had seen some reference to the statement, they had not seen it in full, and freely admitted that nothing could be broader or fairer.

Eventually, the Lawson and other trials were brought up. This gave me an opportunity to state fully the position of our Company and ourselves in regard thereto, and I read the two statements which I had presented to the Commission in Washington on this subject. The gentlemen were greatly surprised at these statements, with neither of which they were familiar, and seemed to be much interested to know that the common report as to our relations to these trials was without the slightest foundation. Before the conference ended, I said to them, "Gentlemen, now that I have stated fully and frankly our attitude in regard to these matters, will you not with equal frankness tell me what, if anything, you think I could do regarding these criminal prosecutions?" Without hesitation, they both said that there was absolutely nothing I could do, that any action on my part would be unwarranted and improper.

We developed at some length the purpose and aims of the industrial investigation of the Rockefeller Foundation. I explained the development of the Rockefeller Institute as analogous. After this subject had been fully set forth, very much to the surprise of our visitors, who entertained to a degree the currently prevailing view in regard to the matter, I said to them, "Gentlemen, if you two and Mr. Gompers and any other important representative of organized labor in this country, in view of the facts which have just been presented to you, say to me that in your judgement the interests of labor will best be served by the temporary or permanent abandonment of this industrial study on the part of the Rockefeller Foundation, I give you my word that I will cast my vote as a Director of the Foundation for the immediate termination of the investigation, and will use what influence I have with my fellow trustees to carry the point." Without hesitation they both said that they would not want to see the investigation abandoned, that from what we had said they believed it gave promise of being of real value and importance to labor, and that they thought it would be most unfortunate to have it discontinued.

After we had developed quite fully these several points, we gave our callers an opportunity to tell us what they had in mind in calling. These three matters seemed to be the things which were on their minds: First, they suggested that in their judgement it would be a helpful influence in the present situation were I to go to Colorado and visit the mines myself and talk with the miners. Secondly, they thought that industrial peace would be promoted and the present feeling of bitterness allayed if a definite agreement were entered into by the Colorado Fuel and Iron Company with its employees, through their own representatives, which would insure to the employees the proper redress of any grievances and satisfactory adjustment of any difficulties; also easy access to the President of the Company in the event of dissatisfaction with decisions reached by subordinate officers. The third point which they made was that it should be clearly stated as a part of this agreement that there would be no discrimination made with reference to members or non-members of the union.

At the first, I took it for granted that what they were driving at was an agreement with the United Mine Workers of America. We discussed the situation very fully, however, and these men made it clear that they did not believe such an agreement was practicable or possible at this time. In fact, Mr. White said to Mr. King before leaving that if such an agreement could be made by our Company with its own employees, they would not ask for any agreement with the union now. They expressed the view that any agreement made should be for a period of years, so as to insure a term of peace and prevent the bringing up for readjustment any matters during that term. We pointed out to the gentlemen how difficult it would be to bring about an agreement between the Colorado Fuel and Iron Company and its men, because of the attitude of the other operators of Colorado, and to some extent because of the attitude of some of the officers of the Company. They recognized the situation, but thought that a great service would be rendered to the cause were such an effort made successfully. They said they would be glad to assist in the preparation of the agreement in any way that we might suggest, but were quick to understand the point which we made, namely that it would be apt to be misconstrued in Colorado were they to have any part in the development of the plan.

The interview was throughout highly satisfactory, and the impressions made on both sides, I believe, entirely favorable. The gentlemen remained to lunch with us, which they were glad to do, and showed every indication of fairness and friendliness.

On Monday, Mr. King and I had a conference with Mr. John Mitchell, who was formerly the President of the United Mine Workers of America and who himself conducted the strike in Colorado ten years ago. Mr. Mitchell is no longer officially in labor circles. We told Mr. Mitchell of the conference which we had had with Mr. White and Mr. Green, of the three suggestions which they had made, and asked him whether he believed that if we undertook to do what they had suggested—a thing which we fully recognize would be difficult of accomplishment—he believed that the United Mine Workers would cease their public agitation and opposition and really do what they could to restore a friendly feeling. Mr. Mitchell found it difficult to believe that these gentlemen would be satisfied, even for the present, with an arrangement made between our Company and its own employees, for he of course felt, as we knew to be the case, that they believed that eventually the United Mine Workers should be a party to the agreement. We made it clear to Mr. Mitchell, however, that we had not misunderstood the attitude of these gentlemen, and I think he saw reasons why, under the circumstances, they would naturally feel such an agreement, if consummated, was a real advantage to the common cause of labor. Mr. Mitchell, after getting the subject fully in mind and after listening to our statement regarding the Lawson matter, our attitude toward the union and the purpose of the industrial department of the Rockefeller Foundation, felt that if we could carry out the suggestions made by Messrs. White and Green, a real service would be rendered, and assured us that he believed those gentlemen and their organization would not undertake to complicate the situation. This interview was in every way satisfactory.

We had hoped to see Mr. Gompers also, but he was unable to come to New York this week. To see these men was a plan which has been in my mind for some weeks and which the other gentlemen all felt was wise. I think we all agreed that real progress has been made.

In regard to the three suggestions of Messrs. White and Green.

First, that I go to Colorado. This, as you know, has been my plan all along, and I am still expecting to leave on Friday of this week, although I am saying nothing about it.

Secondly, that an agreement be made by the Company with its employees. As you know, immediately after the termination of the strike, we put into effect a plan for the selection by the various mining camps of a representative from each, to act as a committee to confer with the management of the Company in regard to matters of common interest. This system has been working with most satisfactory results. Mr. King has talked with all the representatives, Mr. Welborn sees them at the various camps once or twice a month, Mr. Murphy has talked with all of them in person, and Mr. Hicks has talked with all of them. All of these gentlemen found nothing but satisfaction on the part of the men. It has been our purpose from the first to develop the scheme as rapidly as possible and as experience might prove to be wise, in order to insure the permanence of the form of representation, and Mr. King has during the summer worked out what might be called a constitution, outlining fully the relationship between these representatives and the officers, specifying the committees to be appointed to act in the common interest, and clearly stating just what procedure should be followed in the various situations which are currently arising as between the two parties in interest. This plan we had considered during the summer at Seal Harbor and had carefully gone over again with Messrs. Welborn and Hicks last week, all agreeing that it was about in such shape as would be satisfactory and all feeling that its adoption by the men and the officers would go far toward insuring to the men the proper safeguarding of their rights in a way to make it entirely unnecessary for them to seek protection and representation through membership in the union. We had, therefore, practically completed the drafting of just such an agreement as these gentlemen came to suggest, but we did not let them know how far the thing had developed, preferring rather to let whatever might subsequently be done take a new impetus through their suggestion.

Third, we had already provided a clause in the agreement stating that no discrimination should be made among the employees of the Company because of race, religious belief or membership in any organization, union or other association.

You will see, therefore, that these suggestions which they made we were preparing to carry out. The one thing, however, which we feared might prove an obstacle in the way of bringing peace and harmony out of the present situation was that the union might be disposed to regard this agreement which we propose to make with the men as simply a subterfuge and an effort to crowd out the union. In view, however, of the very explicit and definite expressions of Messrs. White and Green, we can proceed now with reasonable assurance of freedom from opposition on that score, and they, on the other hand, will feel that their advice and suggestions have been heeded, and that will be satisfactory to them. Our thought is to have this agreement run for a period of three or five years, if possible. This will insure industrial peace for that period. It will once and for all absolutely differentiate the Colorado Fuel and Iron Company from all the other coal mining companies in Colorado, and that, too, so sharply and clearly that there can be no confusion hereafter. If the plan is adopted within the next month or two, as we expect it will be, Mr. Low's Commission, when it visits Colorado, cannot but report favorably upon it, and the fact that our Company is the only company which has made any real move looking toward the securing to its employees of their rights in a permanent and satisfactory way will redound all the more to the credit of the Company in the public mind.

Of course, we recognize that when this agreement is put into force, if it is lived up to—as it must be lived up to or else be a farce—the United Mine Workers may quietly attempt to unionize all of our employees. This is a danger, however, which we will always be open to, whether the plan is adopted or not, and in the judgment of us all, the danger will be far less with the plan in operation than without it, for if once the employees are thoroughly convinced of the sincerity of purpose of the Company to insure in definite, tangible form to every man redress for any real grievances, a proper regard for his right of appeal and the establishment of a permanent channel of communication between the duly appointed representatives of our employees and the officers, the probabilities of their being willing to pay their dues to the United Mine Workers for not better, if as good, protection of their rights than this agreement will assure them, would seem to us reasonably small. Even if, however, the men should very generally be brought into the union, we will be assured of quiet operation during the life of the agreement, and at its expiration, if the vast majority of the men who have been giving satisfaction as our employees for some years past should prove to be members of the union, it would be a question then for us to consider whether we should not recognize the union, so long as men who are non-union were not discriminated against. I recognize all the dangers which the proposed program lays us open to. We have discussed them fully here and are acting with our eyes open. All things considered, however, we are of the opinion that the course which is planned is, for the present as well as for the future, the wisest and fairest course.

I had thought that possibly I might be able to stop in Cleveland on my way West, to talk with you in person regarding these matters, to which we have been giving such constant attention of late, but it now looks as though that would not be possible; hence this unpardonably long letter. I did not want to go West without giving you the substance of what is in our minds and of what had occurred, that you might be fully informed regarding the situation and what we are hopeful of accomplishing while in Colorado. Mr. King will be with me while I am there, and he and Mr. Welborn both will meet me on my arrival in Trinidad. I need not assure you that we will proceed with the utmost caution in whatever we do, and will take no step which has not been fully and exhaustively considered and which does not meet with the hearty approval of the officers of the Company, as well as the Directors in this office.

I am planning to leave here Friday afternoon. Should you have occasion to communicate with me hereafter, it would perhaps be best to do so through the office, which will be constantly informed of my whereabouts.

Please destroy this letter. As I am leaving the office before it is written out, you will please pardon my not signing it in person.

Affectionately,
John

Forest Hill
Cleveland, Ohio

Although both Rockefellers often suggested that a particular letter be destroyed, the custom seems to have been that most were routinely filed. Ivy Ledbetter Lee was hired by Rockefeller Junior to represent the family during the controversy over the Colorado miners strike. He remained a consultant to the family until his death. Seth Low, a trustee of the Rockefeller Foundation, president of Columbia University, and a former mayor of New York City, headed a Federal commission to study the unrest in Colorado. Clarence J. Hicks, an industrial relations officer of the Standard Oil Company of New Jersey, later became an advisor to Junior. Samuel Gompers was the president of the American Federation of Labor.

---

26 Broadway
New York
October 21, 1915

Dear Father:-

Referring to Mr. Lee's letter of October 14, which I return herewith, and Mr. Mitchell's letter to me of the 20th,—Mr. Lee says this Mr. Inglis is a very high class newspaper man, that he has played golf with many of the leading men of the country and has enjoyed writing these games up for publication. He is an excellent golf player and a charming companion. Anything which he might write he would submit to Mr. Lee and me before publication, so that you can be sure the article would be in every way satisfactory. This being the case, I can see no possible harm in your acting on Mr. Lee's suggestion. Mr. Lee assures me you would enjoy playing golf with Mr. Inglis, and I quite agree with Mr. Lee that whenever, without inconvenience to yourself, the more intimate sides of your character can be presented to the public in a fair and just way, it helps just that much to put you in your real light in the public eye. I should think it an excellent idea to act upon Mr. Lee's suggestion.

Affectionately,
John

Pocantico Hills, N.Y.

William O. Inglis was an Associated Press reporter selected by Ivy Lee to research Rockefeller Senior's career and to conduct interviews with him. Although Inglis compiled a biography, Rockefeller Junior decided against having it published. The transcribed notes of the interviews are at the Rockefeller Archive Center and were published in microform: David Hawke, John D. Rockefeller Interview, 1917–1920, Conducted by William O. Inglis *(New York: Meckler Publishing, 1984).*

---

26 Broadway
New York
February 28, 1916

Dear Father:-

I am sending you an article in regard to my Colorado trip which I think will interest you. It is written by a representative of Medill McCormick's paper, the Chicago Tribune, who arrived in Trinidad two days after I got there. You will recall my having told you that he later said with the utmost frankness that he had always been violently prejudiced against you and me, as had his paper; that he went to Colorado expecting, in the vernacular, to "knife" me, but came away one of my most loyal supporters and ardent friends.

It is interesting to know, incidently, that this man is intending to run for Lieutenant Governor of the State of Illinois this coming year.

No acknowledgement of this letter is necessary.

Affectionately,
John

Golf House
Lakewood, N.J.

Forest Hill
Cleveland, Ohio
September 5, 1916

Dear Son:

Referring to my telegram to you yesterday, as follows:

> "Letter 31st received. My letter of the 28th did not request that you ask Mr. Bosworth to get an estimate and I agree with you that Joe will probably do the work just as cheaply by the day as by contract."

I hope you will understand from this and my letters on the subject that I am entirely willing to leave this whole question with you, and I regret that you have had any bother or trouble about it and the many other things that you have given much careful attention to in your most conscientious desire to everything to relieve me from anxiety and worry. Be assured I appreciate it all more than words can express, and it has been especially gratifying to me since Mother went away, though never for a moment lacking before.

I am grateful to say that I think all our troubles which have been on us in the last fifteen or eighteen months, in connection with the investigations, etc., are out of the way, and I want you to know how thoroughly I appreciate your patience and loyal devotion and unceasing desire to do everything possible in these matters.

I was very much pleased when I heard that you were going

with Chipman on a hunting expedition, and I want your vacation to be a very restful one for you, not only the vacation but the autumn and winter, after the long and trying experiences through which you passed, in connection with the Colorado affairs with which you made such a wonderful success; this is recognized by everybody so far as I have ever heard any expressions, and I have heard many and most gratifying ones.

We are getting along nicely with the office affairs, and it would be impossible for them to have any friction or trouble with us if they desired to, and I believe they do not desire to. We hold ourselves in readiness to do anything and everything for them in any way to aid in carrying out the new programs in the very best of spirit, so that I hope you will dismiss all this from your thoughts.

I have been unusually well and able to attend to business during the summer, and much better than last year, and I hope you will not hesitate to take up with me, or put on to me, anything, at any time, that will be any relief or help to you.

We are having a lovely summer here and will probably delay returning to Pocantico a little longer than we had planned.

Mr. Mitchell has been on about our taxes at Pocantico and goes again tonight. We think these matters are shaping up well and that the officials there are disposed to take up the question in a reasonable way.

I had intended to wait until the first of October before giving you the results of the change of administration at Pocantico, but believing it will be a means of comfort and satisfaction to you, I will give the figures as far as we have gone. During this period of eleven months, the saving in labor and material, that is to say, the expenditures at Pocantico Hills, has been $209,000, and in these calculations we do not include an expenditure of $27,000 made on your house, $16,000 for the new paved road, and other things in connection with automobile purchases, etc., making an aggregate of $50,000. In other words, comparing the eleven months with the same eleven months of the previous years, the aggregate expenditures for labor and materials at Pocantico Hills amounted to $259,000 more than for the eleven months ending September 1st of this year. I desire that these figures shall not be made public. They may vary slightly in some particulars, but they can all be fully confirmed by our books.

With loving regards for you and Abby and each of the dear children, and a grateful heart that you are all spared to me, I am,

Affectionately,
Father

Seal Harbor, Maine

Welles Bosworth was the architect for the Pocantico Hills gardens, a new facade for Kykuit, and for Rockefeller restorations in France.

William S. Mitchell, a Cleveland attorney, was brought to the New York office. He died in 1921.

Kijkuit
Pocantico Hills,
New York
October 25, 1916

Dear Son:

I am giving to you the following securities:

376 Colorado Fuel and Iron Company General Mortgage, 5% Bonds, due in 1943.
7,440 Colorado Industrial, 5%, Bonds, due in 1934.
7,943 shares of Colorado Fuel and Iron Company Preferred Stock.
$400,000 Pueblo Realty Trust Company, 6%, Notes, due in 1919.

I have instructed Mr. Houston to have them all turned over to you at once.

Affectionately
Father

26 Broadway
New York

This gift was valued at $7,968,982.50. Although Rockefeller had given several large gifts to his son in the past, this letter was the first in a remarkable series transferring over $450 million from father to son. Some letters transferred large amounts of cash, up to $1 million; most transferred securities in American industry and government. For example:

American Linseed
United Dye Wood Corp
International Agricultural Corporation
Lakewood Engineering
Atlantic Refining Co.
Vacuum Oil Co.
Standard Oil (NJ)
Standard Oil (NY)

Prairie Oil and Gas Co.
Prairie Pipeline Co.
Illinois Pipeline Co.
Consolidated Gas Co.
Colorado Fuel and Iron Co.
Consolidation Coal Co.
Merchants Fire Assurance Corp.
New York State Bonds
Corporate Stock City of New York
United States Liberty Bonds
United States Bonds

Bankers Trust Company
National City Bank
Equitable Trust Co.

Chase National Bank
Corn Exchange Bank
Manhattan Railway Co.
Interborough Rapid Transit
Wheeling and Lake Erie Railroad
Western Maryland RR
New York Central RR

26 Broadway
New York
November 23, 1916

Dear Father:

The more I have thought about the project which I took up with you last Spring, namely the purchase of the high land at the end of Fort Washington Boulevard, the more the idea has appealed to me. Whether or not I go ahead with the Gothic project which I spoke to you of at the same time, I cannot but feel that this tract of land would make a magnificent addition to the City Park System, and having that in view authorized Mr. Hilton before I came down here to resume negotiations for the purchase of the property on my behalf.

You will recall that you were willing to pay up to $900,000 for the two tracts, and that the lowest price which Mr. Hilton succeeded in getting was $612,000 for the Northern tract and probably $500,000 for the Southern tract—the latter being owned by the Hays estate.

Mr. Hilton advises me by telegram that he has just purchased both tracts for my account, agreeing to pay for the Northern parcel $550,000 or $62,000 less than the lowest price which he was able to get in the Spring—and $21,000 less than the assessed valuation of the tract—and paying for the Southern tract, owned by the Hayes Estate $500,000, which is $73,000 less than its assessed value. As you will recall both of these owners have sought to get these assessment values reduced below the figures named, but were unable to do so, for in each case the City was able to prove the value of the site named by its assessors. I cannot but feel that this purchase is a most advantageous one and hope that you will feel the same.

Mr. C.K.G. Billings owns the tract about the size of these two tracts, and immediately South of them, extending from Broadway to Lafayette Boulevard and including his house and stable. He has permanently abandoned the use of this property as a residence, and although it has cost him Two and a half millions, has named a price of One million and a half for the entire tract. This I learned from Mr. Hilton, who strangely enough has been asked by another client to inquire about the property.

Through Mr. MacLeish, whose son-in-law Mr. Billings is, I have gotten in touch with Mr. Billings, and have arranged an interview with him upon my return to New York. I am proposing to suggest to Mr. Billings the gift of this property to the City for use as a public park. What a magnificent thing it would be if these unique properties could thus be permanently set aside for the benefit of the public!

I am sending this letter to you marked "confidential" because until I have had my talk with Mr. Billings and am ready to have this purchase made public, I am exceedingly anxious that nothing should be known in regard to it.

Affectionately,
John

Pocantico Hills, N.Y.

Junior's purchase of this land in northern Manhattan culminated in Fort Tryon Park and the Cloisters, a medieval museum which is a branch of the Metropolitan Museum of Art. Mr. William Hilton handled most of Junior's New York City real estate transactions. He headed the Empire Real Estate company which Junior owned.

---

26 Broadway
New York
January 18, 1917

Dear Father:

For many years it has been the policy of the office to keep contributions to philanthropic and educational enterprises entirely separate and distinct from any of the business organizations in which we have been interested. I need not mention the reasons which have led to this course and which we have all felt have justified it in the past. More and more I have been coming to feel that we have perhaps erred in this policy and that we have laid ourselves open to the criticism of giving more hitherto to the needs of strangers than to the needs of those with who we are more or less connected through business and industrial relationships. It is perhaps the Colorado situation which has changed my view in this respect. I have felt that to cooperate wisely here and there with the employees of the Colorado Fuel and Iron Company, in the building of a Y.M.C.A. or a church or a bandstand, was distinctly advisable and that the good resulting in the establishing of friendly personal relations and kindly feeling was far greater than the immediate benefit brought about by the expenditure of a definite sum of money. Then too, there seems to me to be not only an obligation to consider the needs of those with whom one is associated, but at the same time there is an added pleasure in helping under such circumstances—a pleasure which I believe is entirely justifiable.

The question of the adoption of such a course as I have above outlined in connection with the Western Maryland Railway and the Davis Coal and Coke Company has been often in my mind. I have discussed it with Mr. Gray, who is sympathetic to it, and we are awaiting developments. I am writing this letter simply to lay before you my view and in the hope that you will give the matter some thought. When we have an opportunity at our mutual convenience I shall be glad to discuss it with you.

Affectionately,
John

Lakewood, N.J.

Golf House
Lakewood, N.J.
January 20, 1917

Dear Son:

Answering yours of the 18th, I do not think it will be necessary for us to have extended discussions in respect to the question of assisting the people with whom we are connected in business relations, but when you have a concrete case to present, we will "crack this nut first" and feel our way along.

Affectionately,
Father

26 Broadway
New York

Hotel Ormond
Ormond Beach, Florida
March 13, 1917

Dear Son:

I am giving you 20,000 shares of the stock of The Standard Oil Company of Indiana, of the capitalization of $30,000,000. I think it best to have the transfer made as soon as possible.

Affectionately,
Father

26 Broadway
New York

---

26 Broadway
New York
March 29, 1917

Dear Father:

There are coming up from time to time opportunities to make contributions toward national preparedness and national defense. I am contributing on my own behalf to these objects. Both Mr. Murphy and I feel that you will want to participate. May we act on our judgment for you in a small way, that is, contributions of not more than $5,000 or $10,000 in any one instance? Prompt action is often necessary.

Perhaps you will be good enough to telegraph your pleasure in the matter.

Affectionately,
John

Ormond Beach,
Fla.

Golf House
Lakewood, N.J.
May 9, 1917

Dear Son:

A brief word only! History is making so rapidly, I can hardly keep up with it, but this fact is being very forcibly impressed upon my mind that my individual ability to do things for others is only a fraction of what it was before the Government took a first mortgage on my possessions and my income, requiring me to pay for governmental purposes many millions of dollars each year. With this in view, we must all reflect very carefully before any further committals are made for gifts of money, especially as I can now see where I shall require to pay in a very few months no less than twenty millions of dollars, not including what I have already paid and for which I am already in debt.

All goes well with us, and we are happy and contented and hope that you and Abby will be rational, restful, retiring, and right minded, and that you will look with righteous indignation upon any overtaxing of your time and strength, remembering that you have much work to do in the world and it cannot all be done in a day. Be patient and be moderate. Allow other people to bear some of their share of the burdens of life, and in the end you will accomplish more, live longer and be happier.

Affectionately,
Father

The Homestead
Hot Springs, Virginia

Washington, D.C.
May 17, 1917

Dear Father:

Your letter of May 14th is received. Abby and I are more pleased than we can say at your acceptance of a Crane-Simplex automobile. My letter in regard to the details of the matter has doubtless reached you by this time. You are right in assuming that there are no orders to be given for both the chassis and the body have been contracted for, but as I said before, Mr. Heydt will arrange to have Phillips make any suggestions on your behalf in regards to details of construction of the body, including color of paint and of upholstery.

Our days in Washington have not been as restful as those at the Hot Springs, for I have been pretty busy with Committee meetings. Then, too, the weather has been close, dark and depressing, but I am through with the work here and we shall be going home in a couple of days.

Hoping to see you in the near future, I am,

Affectionately,
John

Lakewood, N.J.

Junior was a member of the government Committee on Mobilization chaired by A. C. Bedford of the Standard Oil Company (New Jersey).

Kijkuit
Pocantico Hills,
New York
May 28, 1917

Dear Son:

In view of the great prosperity of the Colorado Fuel & Iron Company miners, I earnestly urge that they invest in the company, and I would be pleased to have them for partners.

Affectionately,
Father

26 Broadway,
New York.

---

26 Broadway
New York
June 1, 1917

Dear Father:

In answer to your letter of May 28th, in which you urge that the miners of the Colorado Fuel & Iron Company invest in the Company and state that you will be pleased to have them as partners, may I say that I presume it would be difficult to induce the employees of the Company to invest in the stock, when it has practically never paid dividends, and furthermore that for the Company to urge such an investment or even to suggest it would seem to indicate a foreshadowing of dividends and would at the same time place a responsibility upon the Company which would hardly seem to be wise.

The enclosed bulletin recently issued by the Fuel Company urges the employees, as you will note, to invest their savings in the Liberty Loan. Perhaps at the moment this is the best suggestion which the Company can make to it employees in regard to their use of their surplus earnings.

Affectionately,
John

Pocantico Hills, N.Y.

Forest Hill
Cleveland, Ohio
September 5, 1917

Dear Son:

Answering yours of the 30th:

While I am not familiar with the situation in Colorado, I am very pleased to hear that you are not going West and that you are going to remain at Seal Harbor, and that you have had a very enjoyable and restful summer. This is of more value to you and to me than all the Colorados. You and Abby both needed this summer's rest very much, and I have not heard of anything that has given me so much pleasure as the reports from you of this restful happy period for you both.

I would be very pleased to go to you for a visit. This seems impossible now, and I fear I cannot do so this season.

I am steadily improving. I am in my right mind and possess all my reasoning faculties and enjoying life to the full.

We have had an unusually large number of guests during this summer, and they have contributed to our pleasure.

When Mr. Inglis arrived at the hotel last Wednesday morning, I sent for him and brought him out bag and baggage. He has been here ever since, and looked well and acted well in my dress suit; but his own arrived last night and he looks better then ever. He seems enthusiastic about his work, and we are much together. I do not know how long he wants to remain, but I will be glad to have him stay as long as he thinks he is getting any fish in his net. You will know and judge better of this later on. Meanwhile, I will do what little I can to aid him.

It is alright about the vegetables, and the milk, etc., so long as you all have good digestion. And you know, it would be a lot of trouble to keep the accounts.

I am liking the Crane-Simplex very much, and perhaps I ought to order another, but I have not as yet made up my mind to this.

As to the horses, carriages, etc., I have nothing new. I sent you a little memorandum some months ago regarding this and may want to call it up again in the autumn. My reports are that the coachmen have done pretty well at Pocantico this summer. They certainly ought to do their best in response to the very good treatment they are receiving and have always received from us and the comparatively little work that they are called upon to do.

I am pleased to hear that the second portrait is being copied, and I hope it will be a success. I am wondering how the lady would do whom you employed to paint one of me from the photograph.

I should be glad to begin work with Mr. Sargent here now. Probably I will not go to Pocantico until about the time of your arrival. I do not know where he is, and thus far have not tried to reach him. You may want him for Abby first, and if so, I shall be very happy to have it so. With dear love to each and everyone of you, I am,

Affectionately,
Father

Seal Harbor, Maine

John Singer Sargent, American artist, painted two portraits of John D. Rockefeller, one in the spring of 1917 at Ormond Beach, Florida, and one in the fall at Pocantico Hills.

Forest Hill
Cleveland, Ohio
September 28, 1917

Dear Son:

We sent you and Abby a cake with 1855 marked on it. September 26, 1855, represents the day and the year in which I obtained my first and only situation. We had a nice celebration. Mrs. Eyears and her daughter, Mr. and Mrs. Bustard, Miss Sked, and Dr. Biggar were here. The day was bright and passed very pleasantly.

We are happy that you have all returned safely and hope to join you in a few days. We have made two delays in fixing the date of our departure, on account of some treatments I am having here which seem to be helping me.

With love to you and each of your dear ones, I am,

Affectionately,
Father

26 Broadway
New York

---

26 Broadway
New York
October 2, 1917

Dear Father:

Owing to the purchase of the tract of land on Washington Heights which I made last fall, I am borrowing between $1,600,000 and $1,700,000. In view of the high income tax which is to be levied and of the outgo both for living and for philanthropic purposes which I must count on, my ability to reduce this loan through surplus income during the next twelve months will not be very great. I do not feel that it is wise for me to be in debt to this extent during times which are so uncertain, and am therefore desirous of reducing the debt in part through the sale of Indiana stock.

The market is narrow, the price is considerably off over three or six months ago. I would not contemplate selling over a thousand shares at the outside, and do not suppose it will be possible, even during the period of some weeks, to sell half as much, but after carefully reviewing my various investments, this seems to be the wisest course for me to pursue.

At the time you gave me this stock, its market price was a little below 900, and in giving me instructions at about the same time with reference to the transfer to the Foundation of more of the same stock, you said in your letter of February 19, 1917,—"The current value of this gift in the market today is say 876 a share". I realize that a sale at this time will mean a considerable loss, but feel that it is the prudent thing to do.

I find from the bookkeeping department that no price was given by you at which the withdrawal of this stock from your books should be entered, hence no price has been placed upon the stock in my books. In view of my thought to sell, I should be glad if you could give me instructions on this point now, so that the record of my books will be complete.

Affectionately,
John

Forest Hill
Cleveland, Ohio

---

26 Broadway
New York
December 18, 1917

Dear Father;

In the loss of Forest Hill, I feel as though we had all lost a very dear and lifelong friend. My earliest recollections center there in the old home. What a happy childhood we all spent there. The associations among ourselves and with you and Mother were so sweet, and their memory is so precious. It is difficult to believe that the old house is gone. Even though I have been there seldom of late years, it was always a joy to go back, and not only a pleasure to be there with you, but an added happiness to live over again the earlier days.

I have been wondering what you could do about living there again. The old McCurdy house is the only building which would be in any sense adequate for your use. Possibly that could be made tenantable, at least for the present, until you have decided what to do. If there is anything I can do in the matter or in planning for the future, you know how happy I shall be to render any service possible.

My cold is better, but I am still pretty careful. I was in the house for two or three days last week and went downtown yesterday for the first time. Generally my health is first rate, and the rest of the last few days has put me in good condition. We are expecting to go to Tarrytown on Friday for over Christmas and part of the next week, and are hoping that your plans may bring you back there by that time.

Mrs. Evan's message the other day, suggesting that I come to Lakewood, was much appreciated. I would have enjoyed doing so, but it would not have been possible.

Hoping to see you soon, I am,

Affectionately,
John

Lakewood, N.J.

---

26 Broadway
New York
December 19, 1917

Dear Father:

Several years ago I suggested your giving Dr. Simon Flexner $50,000 as a mark of appreciation of his signal service to the Institute and so as to provide a little ampler living for his growing family. His salary is $12,500. Recently I spoke of the matter again. The more I think of it, the more I feel that this would be a very gracious act on your part and one fully justified by what the Doctor has done and is doing. Dr. Carrel was not long since awarded the Nobel Prize for scientific achievement, which prize is $40,000 in cash. Dr. Flexner's work has been as important in its contribution to advanced medicine and the prevention and cure of disease as Dr. Carrel's. It simply has been perhaps less spectacular. Then too, Dr. Flexner is rendering a tremendous service, quite aside from that rendered to the Institute. He is a member of the Rockefeller Foundation, the China Medical Board, the International Health Commission. He gives much time to these different enterprises, and in addition we consult him on a variety of other subjects. Because of the prominent position into which his own work and these different connections bring him, he is obliged to live on a scale and entertain in a manner which is not true of the less conspicuous men in the Institute. All of this means added cost.

Dr. Buttrick receives a salary of $12,000. Abraham Flexner the same, also Dr. Vincent and Mr. Fosdick. The salaries of all these gentlemen have been at this figure for a relatively short time. Dr. Flexner's salary has been $12,500 for a number of years.

I have talked this matter over again with Mr. Murphy and he is in heartiest sympathy with it. I do hope you will give it favorable consideration.

Affectionately,
John

Lakewood, N.J.

Dr. Simon Flexner was the Director of the Rockefeller Institute for Medical Research since its founding in 1901. Dr. Alexis Carrel was a researcher at the Institute. He won fame for the development of an antiseptic solution and as a surgeon.

Wallace Buttrick was the secretary and later chairman of the Gen-

eral Education Board. George E. Vincent was president of the Rockefeller Foundation.

Golf House
Lakewood, N.J.
December 21, 1917

Dear Son;

Answering your letter of December 19 regarding the gift to Dr. Simon Flexner, might it not be better to increase his salary? We will think carefully and talk further at our convenience.

Affectionately,
Father

26 Broadway,
New York

Golf House
Lakewood, N.J.
December 21, 1917

Dear Son:

Answering yours of the 20th, how would it be to ask Mr. Welborn if he or any others would care to buy any of the stock of the Company and thus cement our relations as partners. In case they do, then we can take up the question of assisting them some, if necessary. You may find it is not necessary—it may be discovered that they are capitalists. However, I would think the first way of assisting them would be to have the company loan them money.

I am, unfortunately, in your sad condition, having desired to help everybody and everything and leaving myself high and dry.

I am hoping, however, that in the years to come I may be able to emerge and wash myself ashore with a cake of Pear's soap.

I have met with large losses on my securities, and I am very desirous to husband my cash with the hope to recoup some small part, at least, of these losses.

Affectionately,
Father

26 Broadway
New York

Denver, Colorado
June 6, 1918

Dear Father:

We have finished our tour through the mining districts and reached Denver late last night.

We are more than gratified with what we have seen in the camps and with the spirit which is universal among the employees as well as the officers of the company.

We have spent a couple of days in Pueblo, have been through the steel mills, where about 6,000 men are employed, have met the representatives of the employees both at a luncheon where an equal number of officers were present, and also in a subsequent meeting with the representatives alone. On both of these occasions the representatives expressed their cordial endorsement of the plan of industrial representation and with full appreciation of it.

I spoke to an audience of over 1,000 people in the largest hall in Pueblo one evening, one-third to one-half of whom were employees of the Fuel Company's steel mills and their families. A most cordial welcome was accorded us.

Abby and I, although a little tired at the moment, are in the best of health and feel well satisfied with our trip so far.

I have definitely arranged to speak at Chautauqua on August

10th, which will mean that I will be obliged to come down from Seal Harbor to keep the engagement. I mention the matter at this time, for one of the chief reasons which has led me to make the engagement was that, in coming down, I should have the opportunity of seeing you in Pocantico. I am hoping, therefore, that your plans for the summer will so work out that you will be at Pocantico just before or just after the 10th, so that I may spend a night with you there.

Affectionately,
John

Golf House
Lakewood, N.J.

Golf House
Lakewood, N.J.
July 10, 1918

Dear Son:

I am giving you 166,072 shares of the stock of the Standard Oil Company of California.

I have directed the office to have this stock transferred to you.

Affectionately,
Father

Seal Harbor, Maine

Golf House
Lakewood, N.J.
July 30, 1918

Dear Son:

I am this day giving you 18,800 shares of the Common stock of the American Linseed Company and 22,400 shares of the Preferred, and 500 shares of the Lakewood Engineering Company, 4,200 shares of the International Agricultural Corporation Preferred and 12,423 shares of the Atlantic Refining Company and 37,269 shares of the Vacuum Oil Company and 13,000 shares of the Standard Oil Company of New Jersey, and I have requested Mr. Houston to have the same transferred to you.

Affectionately,
Father

Seal Harbor, Maine

Seal Harbor, Me.
August 1st, 1918

Dear Father:

Your letter of July 30th, telling me of the securities which you have given me, came last night, and quite overpowered me.

I was only just beginning to fully realize the significance of the previous gift, which you made me just before I left Pocantico, and now this further gift of equal magnitude has come.

Dear Father, I thank you from the bottom of my heart for your great generosity, and this further evidence of your confidence and affection.

The opportunities for doing good which you have made possible to me are unlimited and wonderful.

I can only hope and pray that I shall be as conscientious in my stewardship as you have always been in yours, and I shall strive to be as wise and generous.

In the hope that you may never have cause to regret having placed this great responsibility upon me, and again with profoundest thanks and truest love, I am,

Affectionately,
John

Golf House
Lakewood, N.J.

Golf House
Lakewood, N.J.
September 12, 1918

Dear Son:

Answering yours of the 9th, you could not have enjoyed the visits of the past two weeks which we have had together more than I did.

You are very busy, but you never seem too busy to put yourself out to come and visit me. These visits I appreciate more and more, and I don't tell you so nearly as much as I ought to.

What a Providence that your life should have been spared to take up the responsibilities as I lay them down! I could not have anticipated in the earlier years that they would have been so great, nor could I have dreamed that you would have come so promptly and satisfactorily to meet them, and to go beyond, in the contemplation of our right attitude to the world in the discharge of these obligations.

I appreciate, I am grateful, beyond all I can tell you. There is much for you to accomplish in the future. Do not allow yourself to be overburdened with details. Others must look to these. We will plan and work together. I want to stay a long time to help do my part. I hope you will take good care of your health. This is a religious duty, and you can accomplish so much more for the world if you keep well and strong.

Affectionately,
Father

26 Broadway
New York

---

26 Broadway
New York
November 9, 1918

Dear Father:

Among the oil men whom I met the other day in Mr. Bedford's office, when I spoke about the United War Work Campaign, was Mr. Sinclair. He and his wife came to a musicale in the interest of the campaign at our house a few days later and I had a further pleasant conversation with him there. Subsequently he wrote me a letter, of which I quote the following:

> "At the Petroleum Meeting last Friday, our chairman Mr. A.C. Bedford, suggested that your father might find time to attend one of the meetings. I sincerely hope this will be possible, for even a few words of counsel and encouragement from him would be highly valued, because it is recognized that to his genius for work and for organization must rightly belong much of the credit for the petroleum industry's preparedness when the world was plunged into war."

Mr. Sinclair is a member of one of the teams in our campaign. I saw him at a dinner of the teams last night. He mentioned again his earnest hope that you would sometime meet the Petroleum men. I told him that you were seldom in the city, whereupon he said, "We would gladly go to his home." I replied that that was a new thought to me and that I did not know but what that could be arranged.

I do think it would mean everything for the permanent harmonious relations among the oil people in the country in the future were you to arrange to meet these gentlemen. Could it not be done at Pocantico? Could they not come up there immediately after lunch some afternoon, in automobiles, if that seemed the easiest way, spend an hour with you, and then come back.

I had hoped to talk the matter over with you this weekend but am disappointed that I can not get away from New York to spend Sunday at Tarrytown.

Affectionately,
John

Pocantico Hills, N.Y.

Alfred C. Bedford was a director of the Standard Oil Company of New Jersey and a member of the manufacturing committee. Harry F. Sinclair was president of the Sinclair Crude Oil Purchasing Company.

---

26 Broadway
New York
December 18, 1918

Dear Father:

I had an hour's talk with Mr. Bedford and Mr. Teagle regarding a very important matter connected with their Company, about which I think they ought to talk with you personally and at your early mutual convenience. These gentlemen could not go to Lakewood until Friday, and I have arranged with them to go down on the train leaving here at 5 o'clock Friday evening, and to return on Saturday morning, if this proves agreeable to you. They have engagements earlier and Mr. Teagle wants to go to Cleveland Saturday afternoon, so that this is about the only time they could come. They suggested staying at the hotel, but I told them I thought you would be glad to have them stay with you. If the house is full they will gladly go to the hotel.

Unless I hear from you to the contrary, they will come down on the 5 o'clock train from here Friday afternoon, to spend the night with you.

Affectionately,
John

Lakewood, N.J.

Ormond Beach
February 6, 1919

Dear Son:

I am giving you 50,000 shares of the stock of the Standard Oil Company of New Jersey. I have written Mr. Cary to deliver the same to you.

Affectionately
John D. Rockefeller

26 Broadway
New York

---

26 Broadway
New York
February 11, 1919

Dear Father:

Once more my breath is taken by the receipt of your letter of February 6th announcing the stupendous gift of New Jersey stock which you are making to me. I need not tell you how deeply I realize the great responsibility which each of these gifts brings, for every day of my life I realize more fully the peculiar obligations which rest upon those of large means. A sense of the burden of the responsibility which, through your great generosity has come so rapidly to me during the passing years, would be almost crushing were it not offset by the vision of the wonderful opportunity for useful service which comes with the responsibility.

I appreciate more and more each day what your wisdom and intelligence and broad vision in giving has meant to the world. I realize increasingly the tremendous value that attaches to your endorsement of an enterprise, business or philanthropic, and I need not assure you that it will be my great pride, as well as my solemn duty, to endeavor, while emulating your unparalleled generosity, to live up to the high standards of intelligent giving which you have set. Whenever I am discouraged because of the littleness and the meanness and the petty jealousy of men I find renewed courage as I contemplate your patience, your bigness of heart, your Christian tolerance. Whenever I am oppressed with the feeling that one man can do so little even when he is doing his utmost, I only have to review the marvelous accomplishments of your extraordinary life in order to be heartened for the task which lies before me.

May the God who has led you so wonderfully during all of these years of your life, Whom you have served so faithfully and untiringly, lead me in the same path of duty and of service, and help me to carry on worthily the works for mankind which with marvelous prevision you have so solidly and wisely established.

I thank you, dear Father, for this great gift, and for the continued confidence in me which it implies. May God bless you and help me to live up to the high ideals which have guided your life.

Lovingly,
John

Ormond Beach, Florida

26 Broadway
New York
February 12th 1919

Dear Father:

Charlie Millard sat opposite me at the Brown Alumni dinner the other night. I asked him what the conditions of non-employment of returned soldiers and sailors at Tarrytown were. He told me a committee had been appointed by the Village to deal with the situation and that he had been made Chairman of the Committee. He further said that a number of men had been placed, but there were many of all grades seeking employment.

I volunteered a suggestion that possibly we might find good men for different positions at Pocantico from this group, and I said I would inquire whether we had any such needs.

I feel very strongly that one of the best ways in which to avoid uprisings and disturbances in this country during the next few months is to see to it that the men returning from the War are re-employed, preferably in the positions which they left, as rapidly as possible. Obviously where this is not the case a cause for dissatisfaction and fertile soil for the agitator is the result.

The Standard Oil Company of New Jersey has adopted as its policy the re-employment of all its old men in so far as that is possible, even if they are not absolutely necessary at the moment. This includes the employment of wounded or maimed men who are fit to work. The particular task to which each is assigned being selected having in mind his physical limitations.

Judge Gary told me confidentially that the Steel Corporation is following this same policy. It seems to me to be a vitally important one.

I am wondering whether you will not think it a contribution to the solution of one of the great problems of the day, to employ at P.H. skilled or non-skilled men returning from service in so far as present work exists for them, or work which could well be done, can be undertaken. May there not be road buildings which have been waiting adequate labor? Forestry work which could be desirable? Clearing of fields for cultivation, which have lain fallow. The completion of your water works and adequate roads around them, which can now be entered upon? I present the matter for your consideration in the belief that it is worthy of prompt and generous action.

Affectionately,
John

Ormond Beach, Florida

Ormond Beach
February 18, 1919

Dear Son:

Answering yours of the 12th, I agree with you about the importance of doing the right thing toward the soldiers who are returning home, in aiding them to secure positions. I hear that not a few of them are expecting something better than their old positions and will not be content to return to their former locations, etc., etc., so that I assume great care will be required to be exercised in dealing with each individual case. I want to do fairly and liberally toward the men, but not to weaken or pauperize them by doing any unreasonable things, perchance catering to unreasonable whims, if there be such.

The situation at Pocantico at present is rather difficult. You may surmise what I have in mind when I recall a conversation which we had before my coming away, and on account of this it will not be easy to enter upon new undertakings—some little delay would necessarily be occasioned. I am desirous that we should do all that we ought to do in this connection, but I also hope we can avoid having saddled upon us unreasonable men claiming continuously high wages and demanding the least of service. I could prefer much that we might go slowly and let the natural settling process have its effect and the men come, one by one, as individual applicants and make their arrangements on their merits, subject to removal when their services were not required for any cause.

I wish you might find it convenient to talk with Mr. Ellis on the subject without requiring him to take any immediate definite action, and write me what views he expresses in regard to the interests of the situation, and anything else of interest that he may present in this connection.

Meanwhile I am giving the matter careful thought, and have written him.

Affectionately,
Father

26 Broadway
New York

---

26 Broadway
New York
March 12, 1919

Dear Father:

I have you letter of February 18th, in answer to mine of earlier date, regarding the employment of returned soldiers at Pocantico. Last week I talked again with Mr. Ellis on this subject. It is neither his thought nor mine that soldiers should be employed indiscriminately or in large numbers, but rather that whenever one applied who seemed qualified to do such work as the place might require, Mr. Ellis would be free to employ him.

The spring is so early that work can be undertaken sooner than usual. Mr. Ellis is ready to add to his force from time to time, and in addition to laborers, is especially in need of some painters. He tells me, however, that his orders are to employ no new men, for the present. I hope it may seem wise to you to permit the judicious employment of soldiers, where additional help on the place is needed.

Affectionately,
John

Ormond, Fla.

---

26 Broadway
New York
September 12, 1919

Dear Father:

The receipt of notice from the office of a gift of a thousand dollars from you, marking the anniversary of Mother's birthday, is received with deep appreciation. We do not need the recurrence of these anniversary days to bring vividly into our thoughts the dear Mother, around whom our family life centered so joyously for so many years. I have thought of her so much of late, and have so frequently wished that I could go to her for counsel and advice in regard to some of the perplexing problems that arise. How wonderfully sane and sound she was in her judgments, how just, and always how kind. The debt of gratitude which we owe her grows larger as we go on in life, and our thanks to the good Father who spared her to us so long are ever lifted anew.

With truest appreciation of the gift, I am,

Affectionately,
John

Pocantico Hills, N.Y.

Golf House
Lakewood, N.J.
November 20, 1919

Dear Son:

I am this day giving you 50,000 shares of the common stock of the Standard Oil Company of New Jersey.

Affectionately,
Father

26 Broadway
New York

---

26 Broadway
New York
November 24, 1919

Dear Father:

Your brief but meaningful letter of November 20th, advising me of a still further gift of Jersey stock, is received with profound gratitude and appreciation.

What is there that I can say in the face of such unprecedented and continued generosity? Truly, words are utterly insufficient to express the feelings that this further evidence of your fatherly love and confidence stir in me. I can only hope that the things which I do and the service which I seek to render to my fellowmen may lead you to feel that you have acted as wisely as you have generously.

I thank you from the bottom of my heart.

Affectionately,
John

Lakewood, N.J.

---

26 Broadway
New York
January 22, 1920

Dear Father:

I stopped in at Uncle Will's house early Tuesday morning, he having arrived late the afternoon before. He and the children were in the dining room together. Uncle spoke so sweetly of your having come to Savannah with him, and was greatly comforted by your presence. He is as brave as he can be, but how inexpressibly lonely!

A simple funeral service was held at the house yesterday morning at half past ten, only the immediate family being present. I asked Percy the day before whether they would like to have us go to the cemetery or not. He gave me to understand that they would go quietly just by themselves, and therefore we did not arrange to go.

I hope you got back to Ormond without having caught cold or getting too tired.

Your telegram of the 20th is much appreciated. Abby is gaining every day, and I am trying to be wise and prudent.

Affectionately,
John

Ormond Beach, Florida

Almira Goodsell Rockefeller, William Rockefeller's wife, died on January 17, 1919. Four of her children lived to maturity: Emma Rockefeller McAlpin, William Goodsell Rockefeller, Percy Avery Rockefeller, and Ethel Geraldine Rockefeller Dodge.

26 Broadway
New York
February 2, 1920

Dear Father:

I am happy to know that the clock has been received and that it is so satisfactory. I hope the painted decoration to hang above the mantel will prove equally to your liking.

Aunt Lute continued all of last week to be very ill. Toward the end of the week her lungs began to clear up. But the doctor feared her strength would not hold out. He looked for the crisis on Friday night or Saturday. It came Saturday, and Aunt is much better. She had the best night Saturday night that she has had in weeks, and things are looking most hopeful.

I went to Pittsburgh Friday night to speak at a dinner Saturday night of the Interchurch World Movement, at which were gathered men from all over the United States. The Governor of Maine also spoke, and I had the pleasure of sitting next to him. He is a magnificent young man, one of the finest I have seen. They tell me that in his campaign for election as governor he said that now that prohibition had become the law of the land, he intended to enforce prohibition in the State of Maine if it took the state Militia to do it. Large, fine looking, with a splendid voice, modest and quiet, the young man seems to me to give promise of being a coming leader of men.

We have had six of the servants in our house ill in bed with influenza the past week. Gradually they are improving. Three of the children have also been ill, but all except Laurance are now out, although not fully recovered. Abby is making progress slowly, but finds that her strength does not quickly return. We greatly enjoyed seeing Mrs. Evans, and hope that you did not suffer by her absence.

Affectionately,
John

Ormond Beach, Fla.

Aunt Lute, Lucy Spelman, was the sister of Laura Spelman Rocke-

feller. After Laura's death in 1915, Lucy was Rockefeller Senior's hostess for several years. After her death in 1920, her place as hostess was filled by Mrs. Fanny Evans, a cousin from Ohio.

The Interchurch World Movement was an effort by 31 Protestant denominations to raise one-third billion dollars to promote their common work. The effort raised over $170 million but failed to promote unity among the denominations.

---

26 Broadway
New York
February 16th, 1920

Dear Father:

I am having sent you from Tiffany's two gold safety pins, which Mr. Yordi thought you might find useful with your Golf collars. Please accept them in remembrance of the two delightful visits which Babbie and I paid you this Winter.

Affectionately,
John

Ormond Beach

Ormond Beach,
Florida
February 17, 1920

Dear Son:

I am this day giving you $65,000,000, par value, of United States Government First Liberty Loan 3 1/2% bonds.

Affectionately,
Father

26 Broadway
New York

---

26 Broadway
New York
February 17, 1920

Dear Father:

A long time has passed since I have given utterance to the thoughts so frequently in Abby's mind and mine of our deep appreciation of the many things which come to us through your generosity and which go to make our lives each day so much happier, easier, more comfortable and enjoyable than they would be otherwise. The continued use of Abeyton Lodge, so conveniently enlarged and so comfortably refurnished, the enjoyment of the place at Pocantico which is so dear to us, the privilege of sharing with you the farm products, eggs, milk, cream, poultry, etc., the flowers and plants from the greenhouse, which all winter make our house in New York beautiful, as well as adorning the house at Pocantico, the horses, which are as great a pleasure to me as ever, and the electrics in town, which are such a convenience,—for these and many other things we are daily indebted to you.

Please be assured, dear Father, that our lack of spoken appreciation is no indication of a lack of heartfelt gratitude for the countless evidences of your love with which we are surrounded. It is the little things in life which make for happiness, and so it is these many little things which play so large a part in filling our cups so full of pleasure and joy.

Accept then, this word from Abby and me, not as an adequate expression of thanks, but only as an indication of the channels in which our grateful thoughts are so constantly traveling.

Affectionately,
John

Ormond Beach, Florida

Ormond Beach,
Florida
February 23, 1920

Dear Son:

Answering yours of the 17th, you are constantly thanking me. You are most appreciative and never fail to show your appreciation, and you are just as welcome to anything and everything that you have had from me as you are appreciative.

With tenderest love for you all,

Affectionately,
Father

26 Broadway
New York

---

26 Broadway
New York
May 2, 1920

Dear Father

The housing problem I understand is a very serious one at Pocantico. It is difficult enough to keep good men even when we can supply reasonably comfortable homes. Without the latter the difficulty is increased. I think we will also be obliged to develop the recreational facilities in Pocantico as an added attraction to hold resident workers. Mr. Nelson has some good ideas along this line, which I shall want to discuss with you.

You will remember Abby and I once suggested converting the Scheu house into a Neighborhood Center. Abby has since suggested why not buy Mrs. Moore's old saloon and use it either for a Neighborhood House or for two or three family apartments. It will take a long time to build anything. If this house could be bought for anything short of an exorbitant price, is not the idea well worth considering? If you feel so, perhaps you will start the machinery to work at an early date to see what can be done.

Affectionately,
John

Lakewood, N.J.

PS Many thanks for your birthday present of $100 to Winthrop, of which notice has just been received. Winthrop will doubtless write you himself. In the meantime, this word of truest appreciation from Abby and me.

Golf House
Lakewood, N.J.
May 25, 1920

Dear Son:

I want you to feel free at all times to confer with me with reference to any of your business matters. It will always give me pleasure to be of any service to you, and I hope you will not hesitate to call upon me, as I feel the deepest interest in all your affairs, and will be happy if I can contribute from my own experience at any time anything that would be of the slightest assistance to you.

Affectionately,
Father

26 Broadway
New York

Golf House
Lakewood, N.J.
May 29, 1920

Dear Son:

I am this day giving you 186,691 shares of the stock of the Standard Oil Company of New York. I have directed Mr. Cary to have the same delivered to you.

Affectionately,
Father

26 Broadway
New York

En route
May 31, 1920

Dear Father:

Our trip thus far has been most delightful. We have a beautiful car, very comfortable, convenient and with good men.

After breakfasting on the car Sunday morning in Cleveland we went to the hotel for a moment and then motored to Rocky River. We were delighted with the beautiful residences on the way and, returning, reached the church for the morning service. Only a few of the people whom I knew were at church,—Mrs. Osborn, Jean and Will, Mr. and Mrs. Reynolds, Miss Etsensperger, and one or two others. We then drove by 33 Cheshire Street and up to 997. We went all through the old house and it was most interesting.

Our next stop was for a few moments at the cemetery, where we placed flowers on Mother's and Aunt Lute's graves. When we reached Forest Hill Mr. Sims, Mr. Smith and Pat awaited us at the gate. We had our lunch in the Superior Street Valley by the stream, building a fire and cooking our chops. Mr. Smith had very kindly made us some ice cream which he brought to us. The children were most enthusiastic about the place, thinking it the most beautiful place they have ever seen. Instead of driving about the surrounding country and parks they begged to be allowed to stay all afternoon and have supper in the woods as well, so I went to Mrs. Smith's house—she kindly supplied us with some things and with delicious milk,—and then I went to a bakery and bought a few other things with which, all together, made up a fine supper eaten by the little boat house. The children loved the boat and the rowing on the lake and hated to leave the place.

We got back to the car a little after eight, all feeling that we had never spent a more delightful day.

Forest Hill looks so strangely without the homestead. Nothing but the cellar is left, and yet the children loved the place so much that they wondered that you did not build a bungalow there. I am not perfectly sure if you were to build that you would want to place a house on the same spot because the smoke and the factories are so much in sight towards the lake and the city. The place is really lovely and has the same old charm. Everyone asked about you most affectionately.

We are reaching Chicago this morning to lunch with Dr. Judson and then go on tonight to Omaha, where Mr. Gray joins us and takes us over his road to Denver.

We got good news from Winthrop, who seems to be doing well inspite of the measles.

With a great deal of love from us all,

John

Golf House
Lakewood, N.J.

Dr. Harry Pratt Judson was president of the University of Chicago and trustee of the Rockefeller Foundation.

Denver
June 20, 1920

Dear Father:

The children have done splendidly under Dr. Amoss' careful attendance. Babbie has been up and out for two or three days, although she was the last to come down. Laurance is also about and entirely well, and Nelson is going out a little but still shows some signs of his late illness. We have gotten on admirably in the hotel, have had two good trained nurses and have everything to be thankful for.

John and I have spent the past week visiting the mines, steel mills, and motoring around the beautiful mountain country. We motored over 700 miles during the week and returned here last night.

We are leaving tomorrow, Monday night, and shall go directly to San Francisco. While there I feel that I should see Mr.

Kingsbury, President of the California Company, who is urging me to see him, doubtless in regard to the matters which we had up in New York before we left. From what Mr. Murphy has written me it seems highly desirable that I should have a full frank and intimate talk with him, with a view to getting at the foundation of the facts and in the hope of our reaching some kind of a mutual understanding. Your letter of May 29th is helpful and I will have it in my mind in my talk with Mr. Kingsbury. Thus far he and his associates have simply made general demands. I think I must discuss with him their requests in specific terms both as to men and accounts. Doubtless, as Mr. Teagle said, Mr. Kingsbury is simply throwing up a barrage as a preliminary to the negotiations. What we need to do is to see eye to eye and get the cards all spread out on the table.

We shall be in San Francisco for two days and shall spend Sunday at Pebble Beach, near Monterey, and go Monday to Santa Barbara for a week, thereafter carrying on the trip pretty much as originally planned.

In spite of the annoyance of our illness we are fortunate to have gotten through so well and shall feel all the safer as against the inevitable exposure of travel from now on.

Recalling so delightfully your birthday last year we shall regret the more not being with you and you have our good wishes.

Many thanks for the birthday check for David, which his parents greatly appreciate in his behalf.

With love from us all, I am,

Affectionately,
John

Golf House
Lakewood, N.J.

Between May 26 and August 4, 1920, Abby, Junior, and their four older children traveled through the American West in a private railroad car. Three of the children had measles on the trip.

Kijkuit
Pocantico Hills, N.Y.
September 2, 1920

Dear Son

Answering yours of the 14th ult., with reference to the Manship bust, I am not inclined to have Mr. Manship do another, at least at present. I am not perfectly satisfied with the bronze bust. Possibly I may be a difficult subject for a bust. I shall not be adverse to considering the question of having one made if some other man appears, upon whom we can unite.

As to the statue in front of the Tea House, I think it is very beautiful, but as the price is so very high I hesitate, but I will continue the observation and study, and give the matter further reflection.

Affectionately,
Father

Seal Harbor, Maine

The statue in front of the Tea House at Pocantico Hills was purportedly done by the French artist Augustin Pajou (1730–1809). Pajou was the official sculptor for the court of Louis XVI. He was best known for his portrait busts. After Junior's death, curators from the Metropolitan Museum of Art determined that it was not a Pajou original and Nelson A. Rockefeller had it removed. Paul Manship, the American sculptor, also did the Prometheus statue at Rockefeller Center.

Kijkuit
Pocantico Hills, N.Y.
October 22, 1920

Dear Son:

I am giving you a check for $500,000. It will be available for use on Monday next.

Affectionately,
Father

26 Broadway
New York

Kijkuit
Pocantico Hills, N.Y.
October 23, 1920

Dear Son:

I am giving you a check for $500,000. It will be available for use on Tuesday next.

Affectionately,
Father

26 Broadway
New York

---

26 Broadway
New York
October 25, 1920

Dear Father:

Hardly had the ink dried on my letter of thanks for your splendid gift of Saturday before another letter was received, announcing a second gift of equal size.

Again I thank you most truly and most sincerely. There was never so generous, so loving and so thoughtful a father as you are.

Affectionately,
John

Pocantico Hills, N.Y.

Kijkuit
Pocantico Hills, N.Y.
October 28, 1920

Dear Son:

I am today giving you a check for $500,000. It will be available for use at once.

Affectionately,
Father

26 Broadway
New York

---

26 Broadway
New York
October 28, 1920

Dear Father:

What a delightful habit you are forming! This third gift, of which your letter of October 28th advises me, is as acceptable as was the first.

Again I would express my truest thanks. How can I ever make clear to you how much I appreciate your wonderful generosity!

Affectionately,
John

Pocantico Hills, N.Y.

Kijkuit
Pocantico Hills, N.Y.
November 5, 1920

Dear Son:

I am this day giving you $700,000. Mr. Cary will see that check is delivered for this amount.

Affectionately,
Father

26 Broadway
New York

---

26 Broadway
New York
November 8, 1920

Dear Father:

May I tell you again how deeply grateful I am for your further gift, of which your letter of November 5th advises me. I tried to thank you the other night at dinner, but when a son is so constantly and repeatedly overwhelmed by acts of outstanding generosity at the hands of his father, even a full vocabulary is soon exhausted.

Thank you, dear Father, a thousand times.

Affectionately,
John

Pocantico Hills, N.Y.

Kijkuit
Pocantico Hills, N.Y.
November 12, 1920

Dear Son:

I am sending you a check for $1,000,000, with the hope that you will have wisdom and strength to make the very best possible use of it.

With tenderest affection,

Father

26 Broadway
New York

Kijkuit
Pocantico Hills, N.Y.
November 15, 1920

Dear Son:

I am this day giving you $1,000,000, a check for which Mr. Cary will deliver to your order.

Affectionately,
Father

26 Broadway
New York

Kijkuit
Pocantico Hills, N.Y.
November 15, 1920

Dear Son:

I am giving you $500,000 in cash tomorrow morning.

Affectionately,
Father

26 Broadway
New York

Kijkuit
Pocantico Hills, N.Y.
November 17, 1920

Dear Son:

I am this day giving you $500,000. Mr. Cary will deliver you a check for this amount.

Affectionately,
Father

26 Broadway
New York

Kijkuit
Pocantico Hills, N.Y.
December 15, 1920

Dear Son:

I am today giving you $20,688,000 par value in bonds of the State of New York and Corporate Stock of the City of New York, and directing Mr. Cary to transfer and deliver the same to you.

Affectionately,
Father

26 Broadway
New York

Ormond Beach
Florida
December 28, 1920

Dear Son:

Thank you, thank Abby, thank all the young Rockefellers in your command, for the many most beautiful and most acceptable Christmas gifts which have so gladdened our hearts in far away Ormond.

The thought of your untiring devotion and love is a constant and never failing delight and a source of unspeakable happiness.

With tenderest love for each and every one of you.

Affectionately,
Father

26 Broadway
New York

---

10 West 54th Street
New York
December 31, 1920

Dear Father:

We spent a very happy Christmas here in New York, with the tree up in the big nursery and great mounds of presents all about the room for the different members of the family. We missed you and Babby greatly and felt that the family circle was most incomplete without you.

I have meant to tell you that greatly to my regret I seem to have lost the little photograph of myself which Mr. Yordi gave me with the three photographs of the girls to have framed for you. I am so sorry about this, but fear it must have fallen out of the envelope in which I had it with a number of letters, for I have looked everywhere. If I should find it or am able to find a duplicate in any of our albums, I can have it framed later like the girls' pictures and the frame attached to that frame.

We had a most delightful party at our house yesterday afternoon. The guests were some forty young men and women from Mexico, the West India Islands, Central America and South America, who are in New York as students. An extraordinarily bright, intelligent, attractive group of young people they were, most of them working to support themselves days and studying nights. Mr. Gibson played and Miss Grimm sang most charmingly. Dr. Rose came at our invitation and talked about fifteen minutes on the health work which the Foundation is doing in the homes of these young people. We then all sat down for supper at little tables in the dining room, after which and before leaving the tables we asked any of the guests who felt so disposed to tell us where they came from, how long they had been here, what they were doing and what their plans are. This resulted in the most interesting experience meeting. Then one of the young women, from South America, made a beautiful address of thanks to Abby and me, and many of them spoke with deepest appreciation of what you have done for their respective countries. I wish you could have heard what they said, and could realize even in a small way how widely throughout the world your name is known and respected and your work, both in the development of a great industry and the upbuilding of great philanthropy, appreciated. John and Winthrop helped Abby and me receive the guests, and were perfectly thrilled by the whole experience.

The three older boys, John, Nelson and Laurance, are to be baptized Sunday morning. I know you will rejoice at this decision on their part. We only regret that you cannot be present to witness the ceremony.

We have spent a day or so in the country this week and are to be there tonight and tomorrow.

Affectionately,
John

Ormond Beach, Fla.

Ormond Beach
Florida
January 4,
1921

Dear Son:

I was greatly pleased with your beautiful letter respecting the way in which you spent the holiday, with the young men and women from the Southern republics. I think they must have greatly enjoyed the occasion.

We were all made very happy to hear that the three boys were to be united with the church last Sunday morning, and so much regret that we could not have been present on that occasion. How can we be grateful enough for this manifestation of desire on their part to walk in the footsteps of their parents! Our sincere hope is that their lives will give you the joy and support which yours has given to your parents. If so, you will have occasion for gratitude beyond words to express.

We had our little Christmas festival here, with perhaps thirty or forty present, including the children, with a beautiful Christmas tree and many presents. We had music upon the organ and violin, and all were free to unite in the singing, and altogether it was an old time unrestrained joyous festive occasion, with much pleasantry and good cheer.

Of course we missed our dear ones, but we shall enjoy them all the more when we return, and each day makes one less for us to remain away. With the mild winter, we may possibly look for an early return of the spring. If so, we shall not be slow to embrace our opportunity to hurry back.

With tenderest love for each and every one of you,

Affectionately,
Father

26 Broadway
New York

Ormond Beach
Florida
January 10, 1921

Dear Son:

Answering yours of the 6th, I have today wired you as follows:

"I am still strongly opposed to the increasing of dividends of the Standard Oil Company of New Jersey and urge that you use all your influence against it. There will be time enough for this when we find our cash balances increasing instead of decreasing, and we have experiences such as the V.O. and others fresh in mind, where we have paid high rates of interest because of the desire to increase dividends when we ought to have kept the money in the treasury. It will be easy enough to increase the dividends later, when we see that it is all safe, but I am convinced that the conservative policy which we pursued in the old days in the financing of the oil companies is the right one and I am very desirous that we should not depart from it. I shall be perfectly willing to increase when it is apparent that we have sufficient reserves of cash and that we are steadily increasing those reserves, but these are no times for us to waver in respect to holding our money and keeping our concerns strong and not being unduly influenced by a multitude of little men who are moved by a desire for speculation, etc., and whose aggregate interests are the merest fraction of the large conservative holders who want these concerns so managed that the good name which we have for fifty years of careful management established shall be continued."

Affectionately,
Father

26 Broadway
New York

V.O. was the Vacuum Oil Company, later merged with the Standard Oil Company of New York.

Ormond Beach
Florida
January 12, 1921

Dear Son:

Referring to your telegram of the 12th.

I understand you to state that the concern can pay off the preferred and have $800,000,000 left. Is this correct? So far, so good.

But the history of the case is that this concern had a reserve of, say, $100,000,000 in cash, which notwithstanding its large earnings, was exhausted, and $200,000,000, was borrowed, of which all but $130,000,000 was used up, the last I heard.

Now, conceding all you say, and more, and considering the question from the standpoint of the concern itself, which at all times must be the governing consideration, and not the whim of any small individual stockholder, or a desire to make a market to sell this stock, the prime factor is, as I state, to keep the concern strong, prosperous, vigorous, aggressive, on its own feet and on its own merits. Then it can borrow money. Then it can sell stock. But the tail must not wag the dog, and the business must be conducted primarily for the good of the concern itself, and only then will the best interest of every shareholder be conserved. The matter of selling the shares is of no account, in my estimation, when compared to considerations which I have here enumerated. The stock will find a ready sale at advancing prices when its own holders want to buy it rather than sell it, on account of its intrinsic merits, and any effort to increase dividends to sell stock will result the same as putting it on the Stock Exchange, which thus far has been a failure.

It will be time enough to consider increasing dividends when the increasing reserves of cash, with co-ordinately increasing profits, encourage this, but so long as the business increases, and the cash reserves decrease, whatever the profits show, I prefer much to keep the dividends down and not further mortgage ourselves to bankers at high rates of interest, according to modern methods of financing, which, though I trust was the thing for us to have done under the circumstances of the last two years, is nevertheless to be regretted, and the time will come in my opinion, when we will not be proud of this great debt, bearing high interest, with the redemptive clause of 115, when money is again cheap and we have a superabundance of cash, instead of the condition in which we found ourselves in this period of expansion of the business, resulting in the exhaustion of all our cash resources, and the creation of this debt of practically $230,000,000.

Affectionately,
Father

26 Broadway
New York

Ormond Beach
Florida
February 8, 1921

Dear Son:

I am this day giving you 111,135.48 shares of the capital stock of the Consolidation Coal Company. I hope you will be given wisdom and guidance to administer it in the best way, and that it may prove to be a blessing both to you and to the world.

Affectionately,
Father

26 Broadway
New York

Ormond Beach
Florida
February 14, 1921

Dear Son:

Edith seems not to get on well in managing her finances. Mr. Cutler can give you at any time desired some information about her large indebtedness—and this, too, with a gross income which I judge she must have of somewhere between $800,000 and $1,000,000 a year. I have not succeeded very well in aiding her, though I have earnestly desired to do so. I do not contemplate further gifts, and in this connection it occurs to me to suggest to you, and I think I may later on also to Alta, that if you should find Edith at any time, now or later, in straightened circumstances—indeed, I do not need to suggest it—that you would be on the alert to render some assistance to prevent impending disaster.

Experience is a good teacher. Edith tells me she has learned some things. She tells me she will profit by her experience. I do not suggest great assistance at any one time, but I know you will always be ready to, perhaps I may say, chip in, to prevent dear Edith becoming utterly stranded financially—and I leave this as a final record for your tender and most thoughtful and brotherly consideration for our darling Edith.

Only recently I heard that the Chicago Opera organization had called upon her for an additional $100,000, after most liberal assistance already rendered. I also saw in the public prints that she and Harold had contributed in that connection some two millions of dollars toward keeping this ship afloat. So goes the world, and indeed we learn by experience. What fools we mortals be! And Harold's concern, I may say, with or without his consent, recently threw away on the employees, as I have believed and still believe, without warrant, a vast sum of money under the guidance of some impulse of some mortal, living or dead I know not—but an impulse, good, bad or indifferent, whatever it might have been—well, let's call it gone. Threw away a million dollars of precious gold, more or less. And such is life.

Affectionately,
Father

26 Broadway
New York

Bertram Cutler was hired as bookkeeper in the Rockefeller office in 1901. He retired in the 1960s as the head of the investment and accounting departments.

Ormond Beach
Florida
February 23, 1921

Dear Son:

I am this day giving you the following securities:

20,784	shares	Equitable Trust Company
12,800	"	Bankers Trust Company
2,800	"	National City Bank
1,500	"	Chase National Bank
580	"	Merchants Fire Assurance Corporation
460	"	Merchants Fire Assurance Corp. Pfd.
1,056	"	United Dyewood Corporation
172	"	Corn Exchange Bank

Affectionately,
Father

26 Broadway
New York

Ormond Beach
Florida
March 23,
1921

Dear Son:

I am enclosing correspondence in regard to a request from the Arcadia University for me to contribute.

If a contribution is made, I think it better be made by you, with the idea that in case of my passing—which I desire here particularly to state I do not contemplate at any early period, and indeed my chances for long continuance today seem quite as good or better that ever before, and I am happy to make this unqualified record—or in case of my sudden departure unexpectedly at any time it would be better that you, my successor, and most likely to remain much longer than I, should have to do with the tag ends of business affairs, rather than that these should be entailed upon my estate, my desire being that the estate, for all reasons, should be settled as soon as possible after my departure.

Therefore I think that not only this gift, but others of the same character hereafter, had better be taken up and disposed of by you. I approach the question of the gift without any prejudices. I have given to this project earlier, and have no reason to believe that it has not been wisely used, and that the object is worthy of our consideration.

I hope I have made this clear. There is no mystery attached to it in any way, but it seems best that you should attend to it rather than I.

Affectionately,
Father

26 Broadway
New York

Ormond Beach
Florida
April 5, 1921

Dear Son:

I am this day giving you the following securities:

78,013	shs.	Ohio Oil Company;
26,005	"	Illinois Pipe Line Company;
21,040	"	Prairie Oil and Gas Company;
31,560	"	Prairie Pipe Line Company;

Mr. Cary will see that the same are properly transferred and delivered.

Affectionately
Father

26 Broadway
New York

Kijkuit
Pocantico Hills, N.Y.
June 18, 1921

Dear Son:

Answering yours of the 15th, with reference to certain gentlemen calling upon me on my birthday.

I want to assure you I greatly appreciate this kind thought, but my time is so uncertain, and birthdays, as well as others, are so fully occupied, I have no sense of loneliness or lack of companionship or of the best of fellowship, for which I am most profoundly thankful. I have no lonely days. I have no days when I am possessed of a sense of a lack of companionship. How grateful I should be for all this!

So that while I much appreciate the desire of the friends to visit me on that particular day, and while I would be so happy to see them on any day, especially at the time of my golf, I think, as it might entail some little deprivation in some way to them, it is better for them not to take the trouble. I shall see them betimes and enjoy them as ever, and be grateful for all their helpful kindness and thoughtfulness—and much more grateful for yours, and much more conscious all the time of my inability to fully express that gratitude to you.

With reference to my attending the church, I began to attend the Fifth Avenue Baptist Church somewhere between '66 and '70. I could not definitely state the first time, but Dr. Armitage was the pastor and Uncle Will, I think, came to the church either in '65 or '66, and soon occupied a place of importance. I think he was Church Treasurer. Not long after he united with the church.

Affectionately,
Father

26 Broadway
New York

---

26 Broadway
New York
July 28th, 1921

Dear Father:

You have heard from Dr. Woelfkin, Mr. Colgate and others of the recent meetings of the Northern Baptist Convention recently held at Des Moines, Iowa and of the serious effort which a certain group in the denomination known as "Fundamentalists" have been making for the last two or three years to gain control of the Baptist societies.

These "Fundamentalists" as you know, believe in the literal interpretation of the Bible and in other kindred doctrines which men of broader minds and wider vision cannot today accept.

Were this faction to dominate the denomination, it would be a great blow to the denomination and seriously check the forward movement of its various societies. Moreover this contention simply breeds a spirit of criticism and distrust and enmity in the denomination where there should be confidence, accord and cooperation.

These gentlemen have doubtless also told you of the gift of perhaps a million and a half dollars which has recently been made to the Home Mission Society by an anonymous donor on condition that the income from the fund shall be used only for the support of such missionaries and ministers as subscribe to a specific creed set forth by the donor, and upon the further condition that the money shall revert to other interests named if at any time the majority of the members of the Board of Directors of the Home Mission Society do not subscribe to this same narrow and medieval creed.

As you know, Dr. White is the President of the Home Mission Society. He had given assurance to Dr. Woelfkin and others that the final acceptance of this gift would not be brought before the Convention except when all the delegates were present.

It appears, however, that in line with a preconceived plan prepared by the Fundamentalist group, to which Dr. White had apparently lent himself, in spite of his promise to Dr. Woelfkin, the matter was brought up when the great majority of the men opposed to the acceptance of the gift which limited freedom of thought and belief were out of the room, and upon motion of one of the reactionary leaders, a resolution accepting the gift on the conditions imposed was carried.

You will recall that Mr. Murphy and I suggested and you have made your various gifts to the different societies of the Baptist denomination of late years to include a clause that if the money should at any time cease to be needed for distinctly Baptist denominational work, it could be used for work of a similar nature carried on by some union religious body or other body of some such broad character.

The acceptance by the Home Mission Society of the gift above referred to is a step in exactly the opposite direction of the one in which you have been going. If I had ever dreamed that the Home Mission Society would have accepted a gift on such conditions, permanently binding its trustees to the holding of such narrow views, I would have strongly urged you not to make the gifts to it which you have recently made.

The purpose of this letter is simply to apprise you of this situation and to suggest that you and the Memorial and I will all of us need to give serious consideration to these conditions before making any further pledges to any Baptist societies.

Affectionately,
John

Pocantico Hills, N.Y.

Dr. Cornelius Woelfkin was the liberal-thinking minister of the Fifth Avenue Baptist Church from 1911–1922. In 1922 the church moved from 48th Street to Park Avenue and Sixty-fourth Street under the leadership of Dr. Harry Emerson Fosdick, another leading liberal in the denomination. The congregation moved again in 1930 to Riverside Drive where it reformed as an interdenominational church.

The controversy with the Fundamentalists within the Baptist denomination crystallized Junior's thinking and led him to support efforts toward Protestant unity and the liberalism of the Riverside Church.

Peking, China
September 29, 1921

Dear Father:

The dedicatory exercises of the medical school began last Thursday and end this week Thursday. The important public meeting was held this afternoon. I have just cabled you as follows:

> "Formal dedication this afternoon. Your cable received with great enthusiasm. Exercises most impressive and deeply significant. Love."

The Assembly Hall, which seats 500, was filled to overflowing. Admission was only by ticket and hundreds of requests for tickets had been refused. The day was beautiful. The procession, participated in by many distinguished medical and scientific men from China and Japan, the United States, Canada, Great Britain and Europe, all dressed in their academic caps and gowns, with the brilliant colored hoods hanging down their backs, was truly beautiful and impressive. The President of the Chinese Republic was represented by the Minister of Foreign Affairs, who spoke for the President and on his own behalf. Speeches were also made by the Ministers of the Interior and Education. Dr. Vincent opened the exercises by officially turning over the buildings to the Peking Union Medical School and installing Dr. Houghton as the Director of the School. Dr. Houghton then proceeded to introduce the speakers. After those above mentioned Mr. Roger Greene made an admirable address, and my address was the last on the programme. Your cable was most appropriate and was received with prolonged applause.

Of course as is both natural and proper, you are the central figure of the whole enterprise. The expressions which have been made to me personally by the President of the Chinese Republic, who gave Abby, Babbie, Mr. and Mrs. Ryerson and me a special audience of nearly half an hour the other afternoon in connection with the brilliant reception given to all members of the visiting party by the Secretary of Foreign Affairs, an American educated and brilliant man; by the Minister of the Interior and the Minister of Education and the Premier, all of whom I have called upon officially, as well as Mr. Schurman, the American Minister, the British Minister, and the Belgian Minister, all of whom have entertained us, have been indicative of the deep appreciation which is felt to you personally for the great enterprise which you have made possible here. Many delightful personal messages have been entrusted to me by these various gentlemen for you. Moreover, the President of the Republic has sent you through me a decoration of the first order.

Our party has been received and entertained officially in a most distinguished and gratifying way, all of which has brought valued publicity to the college and has helped to interest the Chinese people as well as the foreign population in it.

All feel that the exercises have been far more helpful and satisfactory than was even expected. The enterprise itself is a truly wonderful one. It seems hardly possible that there should now be in existence here, in the midst of the Chinese Republic, a medical school and hospital with buildings, equipment and a faculty second to none in any part of the world, and yet that is actually what is in operation here today.

The officers and the Board of Trustees of the college have been in session half and sometimes all of almost every day for the past week. The budgets for the next three years have been gone over with the utmost care and in the fullest detail. A vast number of questions of policy have been discussed and decisions reached, and I feel that many uncertainties have been done away with, many misunderstandings cleared up, and that the situation is in splendid shape. While it has not been possible to reduce the budget to any material extent, the close scrutiny which we have given it has convinced us all that the expenditure is a modest one in comparison with the expenditure in similar institutions in America, that the money is being wisely and productively used and that the danger of extravagance and undue haste in the development of the institution has been reduced to a minimum.

Dr. Houghton, the directing head of the institution, is one of the finest men in our group. He is able, highly trained scientifically, has been in China as a medical missionary for many years, has a good business head, infinite patience, splendid judgement, a well balanced mind and a spirit than which there is none finer. We all regard him as a truly ideal man for this responsible position.

The influence of this medical school is going to be much more far reaching than we had dreamed. It is already setting the standards for China and its influence is extending even now beyond the boundaries of that country. That incidentally its establishment is sure to be an important factor in fostering friendly feeling toward the United States on the part of China is already very clear.

I think if you were on the ground yourself and had given the whole situation in all its bearings the careful study which the rest of us have during the past ten days you would feel satisfied that the money invested here, although a large sum, will produce rich and constantly increasing returns.

I am enclosing an official programme of the exercises in which you will find on the fly leaf a photograph of the front of one of the buildings. This gives a splendid idea of the character and beauty of all of the buildings.

We leave here on Friday morning for Shanghai, going then to Manila, Hong Kong and Canton, and to Japan where we expect to arrive about the middle of October. Although the days are filled with interesting and important events, and we are grateful beyond expression that we have made this trip, we are nevertheless thinking with satisfaction that about half of the time of our absence from home has elapsed, that within not much more than two months more we shall be with you again.

Never have I more greatly admired the sound basis upon which you have from the outset, organized your philanthropic endeavors, never have I realized more fully the immense amount of good which you are doing, never have I been prouder to be your son than during the past few days.

With a heart full of love and gratitude, I am,

Affectionately,
John

Pocantico Hills, N.Y.

The Peking Union Medical College was a project of the China Medical Board of the Rockefeller Foundation. By 1947 the Board had contributed funds and land to the college exceeding $45,000,000.

Kijkuit
Pocantico Hills, N.Y.
December 12, 1921

Dear Son:

I am this day giving you the following securities:

$4,447,000 United States Government 3 1/2% Bonds due in 1947

$10,523,500 United States Government 3 3/4% Bonds due in May, 1923.

Affectionately,
Father

26 Broadway
New York

Kijkuit
Pocantico Hills, N.Y.
December 17, 1921

Dear Son:

Referring to the purchase by the Consolidation Coal Company of some of their old bonds, why should we not take the position with them that they cannot buy any of their own securities, or any of their own properties, now or at any time, without the knowledge or consent of stockholders who have no interest in their properties. In other words, they cannot trade with themselves without the consent of those who might be disadvantaged by so doing.

Affectionately,
Father

26 Broadway
New York

Kijkuit
Pocantico Hills, N.Y.
December 17, 1921

Dear Son:

I am this day giving you the following securities:

40,000	Shares	Consolidated Gas Company Stock,
40,000	"	Manhattan Railway Company "
10,000	"	New York Central R.R. Co. "
60,000	"	Western Maryland Ry First Preferred
60,000	"	Wheeling and Lake Erie R.R. First Pfd.
$1,000,000		Interborough Rapid Transit Co. 5% Bonds
$1,000,000		Manhattan Railway Co. First Mortgage 4% Bonds
$1,000,000		Manhattan Railway Co. Second Mortgage 4% Bonds

Affectionately,
Father

26 Broadway
New York

---

26 Broadway
New York
December 21, 1921

Dear Father:

Your letter of December 17th, advising me of the further large number of securities which you have given me, brought another thrill of gratitude and appreciation. I tried to thank you the other day when you were here, but words so feebly express the deep feelings which those great and numerous gifts arouse within me.

Princely and unprecedented as these gifts have been, and highly as I value them because of their potentiality for good, they are as nothing compared to the gift of yourself which you are making me each day and have during all my life. I thank the good God every day for my Father.

With deepest gratitude and truest affection,

John

Ormond Beach
Florida

Ormond Beach
Florida
January 14, 1922

Dear Son:

Referring to yours of the 7th, with reference to the Consolidation Coal Company, the question respecting our future relations to this and to other such like interests, I take it, will be governed, to some extent, by the question of whether we can secure men of the right type to represent us.

I take it that with the large amounts of capital we have to invest, if we succeed in securing men of the right kind, we can in a number of cases better afford to own either manufacturing or producing companies and scatter them amongst the banking or that line of investments.

Furthermore, it is to be remembered that you have five sons coming along, and it will not be many years before you will begin to choose places for them to take, for their education; and naturally, for some of them, for their future settled business; although they will in the nature of the case also come to have general knowledge of the affairs which you have in hand, so that they can be of the greatest assistance, jointly with you, in administering the large affairs that have fallen to us.

It seems to me that as a general proposition it would be better for them to turn their attention to work and administration and the care of the property, seeking erstwhile, of course, to cultivate in them the desire to give out as we have sought to do to benefit others with the result of our divided attention, primarily to business, but happily for us, we have from the first kept along with the benevolences and the helpful relations which brings us today so much satisfaction and real happiness. Let us be happy indeed and rejoice in what we have been able to accomplish, giving God the praise—to Whom it is due.

With tenderest affection,

Father

26 Broadway
New York

Ormond Beach
Florida
January 23, 1922

Dear Son:

I am this day giving you the following securities:
800 shares Wheeling and Lake Erie Ry. Co. Preferred Stock
53,961 " " " " " " 7% Prior Pfd. "
71,472.85321 shs Western Maryland Ry Co. First Pfd Stock
19,175 " " " " " Second " "
15,872.048 " " " " " Common "
hoping that you will have the wisdom to manage, supervise and direct in the administration of the affairs of these corporations in such a way as to bring the best results, not only, but that you will be guided in the distribution of any moneys derived from the same in the way that will do the most good in the world.

With tenderest affection,

Father

26 Broadway
New York

Ormond Beach
Florida
January 26, 1922

Dear Son:

As to the sums which I have handed you from time to time, it is to be remembered that I have already set aside large amounts in our different trusts, for benevolent purposes, in addition to my regular giving personally, and with the careful and protracted study which I give to each object of any considerable moment, it is evident that I shall not fulfill to the complete extent, my heart's desire to make everything that I can give to the world available, for many years to come.

As you are in touch with the world from a somewhat different angle from mine, and there have been ample means left by a kind Providence, I have hoped that with your constant and careful studies, and wide and broad knowledge of the needs of the world, you would have the fullest enjoyment in personally determining and carrying out plans of your own for helping the world, and I rejoice to afford you this opportunity, in the confident assurance that great good will result therefrom.

I am indeed blessed beyond measure in having a son whom I can trust to do this most particular and most important work. Go carefully. Be conservative. Be sure you are right—and then do not be afraid to give out, as your heart prompts you, and as the Lord inspires you.

With tenderest affection,

Father

26 Broadway
New York

26 Broadway
New York
April 3, 1922

Dear Father:

The little church at Pocantico Hills is getting on well. It is going to be charming. Mr. Nelson asks whether you will be willing to furnish electricity for the church at the same low rates which you allow for the Lyceum and the bowling alleys. He says Mr. Buswell estimates the cost of lighting the main part of the church at about six cents per hour under such an arrangement, and 18 cents at the regular rate. In addition, the power for the electric stove which Abby is giving, for the clock and the chimes and for the organ would likewise be much less under this arrangement with you. Please let me know your pleasure in the matter.

You will be interested in the enclosed calendar of yesterday's services—the last in the old church. The building was filled and the occasion was one of much sentiment. Next Sunday we meet in the new building.

Affectionately,
John

Ormond Beach
Fla.

26 Broadway
New York
April 17, 1924

Dear Father:

It is gratifying to think of you as at Lakewood, and so much nearer to us than at Ormond. I am sorry not to be coming down at once to see you, but have been nursing a cold for the past week, which, together with some engagements which I have had to meet, has made it seem unwise for me to try to get to Lakewood this week. I am hoping to come down for a night next week, possibly Tuesday night, if that is agreeable to you, but I will telephone later. The cold is better now, and will, I am sure, soon pass by. It has not been serious, only annoying.

The Bayonne labor situation has been a most interesting one. Unfortunately, the newspaper accounts give the public the impression that the appeal to me is a spontaneous, whole hearted appeal on the part of the men employed by the company, whereas in fact it is largely the result of a political move on the part of two or three ambitious politicians among the employees to get publicity for themselves and political prestige as well. The company officers have handled the matter for the Jersey Company in a most frank, open, kindly, patient, and at the same time, statesmanlike manner. I have only words of highest praise for them. Their several meetings with the representatives of the men, meetings planned and carried through as part of the Plan of Industrial Representation, have been most friendly and the facts presented entirely convincing to the great mass of the men. The Vacuum's position is distinctly bad. While they pay the same wages as the Jersey Company, they have resolutely declined to consider the adoption of a plan of industrial representation or any of the insurance and benefit features which the Jersey Company has in effect. The walkout of their men yesterday has forced them to come down from their highhorse and realize that a new day has dawned in industry, and I am earnestly hoping that in the meeting which they are to have with their men today they will agree to the election of representatives by the men and the introduction of such modern methods in their company as have long been in vogue in the Jersey Company. A number of interesting things have happened, which I shall be glad to have a chance to tell you about when we meet.

Hoping that you are quite rested from the trip and none the worse for it, I am,

Affectionately,
John

Lakewood, N.J.

Pocantico Hills
New York
July 25, 1924

Dear Son:

In some of the papers we notice from time to time the statement that after I had accumulated the great fortune I began to give it away. I think that gradually, and carefully, through Mr. Lee or in some other way, this should be corrected, and made to appear as it really was, that in the beginning of the getting of the money, away back in my boyhood, I began giving it away, and continued increasing the gifts as the income increased, and that it was a work of my whole business career and not of the last end.

Affectionately,
Father

26 Broadway
New York

Ormond Beach
Florida
January 27, 1925

Dear Son:

Answering yours of the 20th, outlining your plans for a trip South, and the promise of a visit here, which I do not need to say fills me with great joy and anticipation.

We want you all to come to our house. It would be lovely to have you all here at the same time, and I think there is no doubt but what we can arrange it. I understand Mrs. Evans will, if she hasn't done so already, write you fully giving cordial endorsement of this view.

It would seem too bad to have any of you over in the hotel, and I may say that our floors are of soft wood, and I think the boys would enjoy sleeping on them if there should not be enough beds, but I believe we can do even better than that, and provide comfortable sleeping accommodations in beds. This would certainly be our pleasure.

I am looking forward with eagerness to your coming, and to hearing your account of the different interesting experiences to which you refer. We are always storing up interesting information, which brings us great pleasure and satisfaction.

Affectionately,
Father

26 Broadway
New York

26 Broadway
New York
June 6, 1925

Dear Father:

I am sending you by mail a cravat, which I bought some time ago and meant to have taken it to you recently, but overlooked. It comes with the same return privilege, in case it is not satisfactory, and no feelings will be hurt.

I so thoroughly enjoyed the last weekend, with its several visits with you.

Affectionately,
John

Lakewood, N.J.

Golf House
Lakewood, N.J.
June 9, 1925

Dear Son:

The package—precious package—containing a beautiful and most satisfactory tie, was duly and very gratefully received. Be assured of my appreciation of your unfailing thoughtfulness—and you know my gratitude is always accompanied with the thoughts of favors yet to be received.

All goes well with us here. We have thought much of you during the hot weather, with all your work; but as we are circumstanced, with never a thought or care, and nothing to do but to keep cool at 103 temperature, we came out beautifully, only that the whip-poor-wills insisted upon singing the whole night through. We pursued them with shot-guns, but it made no difference—they sang as much as ever, and we still continue to like whip-poor-wills.

With happiest recollections of our last visit, and tenderest affection for you all.

Father

26 Broadway
New York

Golf House
Lakewood, N.J.
November 10, 1925

Dear Son:

Answering your good letter of the 25th, we sent you yesterday the following message: "Letter twenty fifth received. All goes well and we urge you to stay for absolute quiet and rest. With tenderest affection." This morning we have telegraphed you further: "I advise carefully to consider going to some quiet place in Switzerland, the air is so bracing and stimulating; but this is only a suggestion. Love."

The second message was sent in view of the happy experience of some friends with whom we have just recently been talking. Switzerland seemed to lift them right up, and they found good hotel accommodations. I need not repeat what I have so often said, that the question of health and strength and vigor has so much to do with an active, useful, religious life, that everything else must bend to securing and maintaining it. The slow eating, the discrimination in diet, the sleep, and the independent rejection of many of the numerous social demands are of supreme importance. I attribute my good condition to my almost reckless independence in determining for myself what to do and the rigid adhering to regulations which give me the maximum of rest and quiet and leisure, and I am being richly paid for it every day, and believe I have accomplished more for the benefit of others than could have been done otherwise. Please do not hesitate to stay as long as you think best, and rely upon it, we will keep the wheels moving here, and develop strength and resourcefulness in some of your aides, who will be better for being obliged to act more on their own judgement. You know I have shirked all my life, and, I might say, have done very little that I could get others to do, and have accomplished far more than I could have done if I had pursued the other policy of trying to do it all myself.

We are having a perfectly lovely time in Lakewood, and are building a beautiful fence all around our estate, and we are delighted with it. It is far superior to any fencing we have at Pocantico. I am sure you will be much pleased with it.

We will hope to see Abby and David, and will do our best for them, and for the other dear children.

Give yourselves no concern about affairs here, and rest, rest, rest—and fight, if need be, for freedom from the many who would pull you down instead of helping to lift you up.

With tenderest affection for you and Abby,

Father

Paris, France

---

26 Broadway
New York
April 8, 1926

Dear Father:

We are all so glad to know of the possibility of your coming to Lakewood within the next week or two. Ormond seems a long ways off, and we have seen but little of you during the past nine months. When you are at Lakewood it is easy to spend a night with you from time to time, and when you reach Tarrytown we can hope to see you frequently.

Our trip to Hampton, with all the boys except John, during the Easter holidays was most successful. We lived on the campus for four or five days and came into frequent and intimate contact with both teachers and students. Everyone was most hospitable and kindly. The boys loved the atmosphere and made many friends on every hand. They were profoundly impressed with the seriousness and earnestness of the colored students, both boys and girls, and with the high grade of work which they are doing. They had an opportunity to meet and talk individually with the scholarship students which each of the boys is helping to support, and that also interested them. The visit was well worth while and a real inspiration to us all.

I wish you could have been in the auditorium on Sunday night when a thousand or more students were gathered together to sing their beautiful songs for us, at which time I was asked to say a few words to them. You would have enjoyed just looking into their faces.

After leaving Hampton we spent a couple of days at Richmond, visiting four of the beautiful old places on the James River, all of them historic and charming. We made many friends, who showed us every courtesy, and the two days thus spent were filled with interest.

I am to be in Cleveland on Monday next, to speak at a Phi Beta Kappa dinner that night, and the following night in Pittsburgh to speak at a similar dinner there. I am to have lunch with Anna Nash in Cleveland and shall doubtless see some of the other relatives, as well as to catch a glimpse of Forest Hill and visit the cemetery.

Our western trip for the early part of the summer is well under way and promises to be most interesting. We leave on the 4th of June. Nelson will remain at Pocantico for a week or two after we go, until John is through college, when both boys are sailing for their bicycle trip in France.

Looking forward to seeing you soon, I am,

Affectionately.
John

Ormond Beach, Florida

Among the towns visited on this spring trip was Williamsburg, Vir-

ginia. After this visit, and meeting with Dr. W. A. R. Goodwin, Junior began buying property in the town. By the time of his death in 1960 he had invested over $60 million in the preservation and restoration of the Colonial town.

Anna Nash was the daughter of Franklin Rockefeller, Senior's younger brother.

On the western trip Junior revisited Yellowstone and the Jackson Hole area in Wyoming. His meetings with Horace M. Albright led eventually to his purchase of over 30,000 acres in the area which is now part of Grand Teton National Park.

---

26 Broadway
New York
April 9, 1926

Dear Father:

Our talk at Ormond recently in regard to the motives and circumstances which led to the establishment of your various philanthropic boards and foundations has moved me to make this resume of the salient facts in the situation, thinking it may some time be of value.

The Rockefeller Institute for Medical Research, conceived by Mr. Gates and started with a pledge from you dated May 25th, 1901, of up to $20,000 a year for ten years, was the first of the eleemosynary enterprises which you organized. Its charter was obtained from New York State on May 28th, 1901. The total contributions for principal which you have made to the Institute to December 31st, 1925, amount to $39,904,602.76 The difference between that sum and the Institute's total capital resources on June 30th, 1925, $44,357,393.86 is with the exception of one or two small donations from grateful friends, made chiefly by gifts from the Rockefeller Foundation, which have amounted to $3,000,000.

The General Education Board, established under a Federal charter granted on January 12th, 1903, with an initial gift of $1,000,000, for current needs, was the second philanthropic institution organized. Your interest in negro education and the contributions which you had been making to many negro schools for a number of years through the American Baptist Education Society, led to the serious consideration of the formation of a trust fund of two or three million dollars, to be devoted to that particular object. It also caused me to accept Mr. Robert C. Ogden's invitation to join one of his trips to the South for the purpose of visiting various negro educational institutions. On that trip I met and had opportunity for full conference with many of the leaders in that educational field. The result was the establishment of the General Education Board, with a charter broad enough to cover all fields of education throughout the United States, irrespective of race, creed or color.

Your initial gift to the General Education Board for principal was made on October 3rd, 1905, in the amount of--$10,000,000

Subsequent gifts in 1906, 1907 and 1909 total --20,916,063.80

In 1919, 1920 and 1921 you made three gifts for Medical Education, aggregating ---------------------------------- 45,579,082

In 1919 a gift for the increase of teacher's salaries of-- 50,125,949

Your total gifts for the principal amount therefore, to ---------------------------------$126,623,094.80

In making the gifts for Medical Education and the increase of the salaries of university and college teachers, you indicated that the principal as well as the income was available.

The total appropriations made by the Board to December 31st, 1925, from the principal of these designated gifts amount to $55,418,302.46,leaving an unappropriated balance therefrom of $40,286,728.54

Adding to this balance the total of your other gifts for the principal of ------------------------------------$30,918,063.80 which takes no account of a small balance of $15,025.07 still unappropriated from the moneys given the Board by Mother's estate makes a total net of the principal unappropriated of ---- --$71,204,792.34

Although the promotion of negro education was the original interest of the Board, it shortly concerned itself with education in a broader sense. While it has continued its interest in and support of negro education, by far the largest part of its funds, roughly nine-tenths, has gone into the endowment of universities and colleges for whites throughout the land, and into the promotion of medical education on a sound and scientific basis.

This broadening of the Board's field in the United States suggested the opportunity for service to education in foreign lands, which resulted in my establishing on January 16th, 1923, the International Education Board, with a Virginia charter, enabling it to deal with any educational problems throughout the world and gifts toward current needs of more than $1,000,000.

To the International Educational Board I have contributed for principal -------------------------------------- $20,050,947.50

The Board has made appropriations from principal to December 31, 1925, of -- 186,125

Leaving a balance of principal unappropriated December 31, 1925 of-- $19,864,822.50

The International Education Board has the same president as the General Education Board, it avails of the part time service of some of that Board's officers, its Board of Trustees is largely composed of members of the Board of Trustees of the General Education Board. As time goes on, it would seem desirable that these two boards should function in ever closer cooperation, if indeed a merger or organic affiliation of the two may not some day be desirable. Thus there would result an instrumentality with charter powers to deal with educational problems of every kind not only in this country but throughout the world.

With the establishment of the General Education Board, the field of education in the United States began forthwith to receive full attention so far as our obligations therein were concerned. In the meantime, your own miscellaneous benevolences had been growing and ramifying so that the desirability of the establishment of a fund with worldwide freedom in the eleemosynary field became increasingly evident. Whereupon, on March 14th, 1913, the Rockefeller Foundation was brought into being, with a New York State charter and an initial gift from you of $100,000,000. With a view to having this new foundation provide adequately for these personal gifts which you had been making up to that time, you stipulated that $2,000,000, of the annual income of the fund should be available for such purposes as you might designate, leaving the balance free for such general uses as the Trustees might see fit. This provision, after being in force for several years, was revoked by you, the entire income of the fund falling under the control of the Trustees.

In addition to the initial gift for principal of $100,000,000 made to the Foundation, further gifts for principal were made as follows:

February 28, 1917	25,765,856
December 19, 1919	50,438,768.50
	$176,204,684.50

The total of appropriations from principal made by the Foundation to December 31, 1925, amount to ----------- 11,000,000

Leaving the present principal of the fund, (not including an item of $8,962,154.62 invested in lands, buildings and equipment chiefly in China) ------------------------------$165,204,624.50

The Rockefeller Foundation, originally with the $2,000,000 of annual income, the application of which you reserved the right to specify, and subsequently to a considerable extent on its own account, made contributions to the general philanthropies in which you had been interested and many others in addition. At the same time, there were certain intimate personal enterprises, chiefly denominational and religious, in which you and Mother continued to have a special interest. Thus it came about after Mother's death that you established the Laura Spelman Rockefeller Memorial, in 1918, with a New York State charter, that there might be a continuing provision for such enterprises as these. Your initial gift to the Memorial for the principal was October 8, 1918 --------------------------------- $3,857,170.25

It has been followed by further gifts for principal, totaling ------------------------------- 70,018,287.12

Making a total now on hand of----------------- $73,875,457.37

At the outset the Memorial operated largely in this intimate field, and still does to some extent. However, as its resources greatly increased and as a result of its various studies of the fields of human need, the Trustees have been led increasingly to concentrate their efforts along the line of the social sciences. At the same time, they have continued to have in mind an interest once expressed by you and highly appropriate in view of the memorial character of the fund, in the needs of women and children.

This general trend of the Board towards a rather definite individual field has seemed the more natural and appropriate in view of the fact that with the resources which you have so generously put at my command, I have been taking over increasingly the current family obligations toward local and personal philanthropic and religious and denominational interests.

A summary of the above shows our gifts of principal to these various philanthropic corporations as of December 31st, 1925, to be as follows:

Rockefeller Institute	$ 39,904,602.76
General Education Board	126,623,094.80
International Education Board	20,050,947.50
Rockefeller Foundation	176,204,624.50
Laura Spelman Rockefeller Memorial	73,875,457.37
	$436,658,726.93

Less principal appropriated:

General Education Board	$55,418,302.46	
International Educational Board	186,125	
Rockefeller Foundation	11,000,000	66,604,427.46

Leaving total available principal resources,
aside from the several unimportant
omissions noted heretofore, of ----------------$370,054,299.47

The reasons which led to the formation of each of these boards stand out clearly and sharply. In the pursuance of a lifelong policy, you were feeling your way along in a new and untried field, taking only such steps from day to day as seemed clearly wise and deferring the taking of further steps until they became equally clear and wise. To have brought all these activities into being at one time and through a single organization would not have been possible, at the onset, for the following reasons:

1. Because the wisdom of setting aside substantial sums of money in this way had not be proved.
2. Because you would not have been ready to give such unprecedented sums at any single moment.
3. Because public opinion had not been educated up to the point of understanding and approving philanthropy on so colossal a scale.
4. Because you were not ready to enter a world field then.
5. Because it would have been well nigh impossible at that time to find men big enough, wise enough, experienced enough to deal with so mighty a problem.

At the same time, as you said to me at Ormond, if you were proposing today to set aside for the well-being of mankind throughout the world the total sum of money which has been put into these foundations, you would undoubtedly combine all the activities, with the exception of the Rockefeller Institute—which ought properly to be an independent entity—in the hands of a single board with a charter as broad as the charter of the Rockefeller Foundation. With the soundness of that conclusion I am in complete accord. In the light of the experience of the last thirty years, I am convinced that one representative board with competent officers and staff and with departmental committees of the board to deal with the various fields, instead of the separate boards that now exist, could cover the whole field with ease and economy. Such a plan of organization would result in much saving and the prevention of many overlappings in fields, in which, with the best intention of everyone's part, duplications at least to some extent have been almost inevitable under the present set-up.

Trusting that you may find this resume as interesting to read as I have found it to write, I am,

Affectionately
Your son
John D. Rockefeller, Jr.

Ormond Beach
Florida

Golf House
Lakewood, N.J.
May 4th, 1926

Dear Son:

I have read with much interest your letter of April 9th, summarizing certain matters which we have talked over on the occasion of your visit to Ormond, during the winter.

As I again review our philanthropic gifts during the past thirty years, I feel we did well to proceed slowly and cautiously as we did. If the whole thing were to be done today, you have rightly understood me as feeling that it should be done, and doubtless could be done, through a single organization, with many economies and the avoidance of such overlapping as you point out. It may and very likely will be wise, if not in the immediate future, a little later on, to bring some or all of these boards themselves, certainly various of their departments, into closer cooperation and affiliation. As rapidly and as fully as such steps become wise and desirable, their being taken would seem to me eminently appropriate and advisable. While the management of these funds is wholly in the hands of the several boards of trustees, because I regard this matter as so important for the best accomplishment of the purposes for which the funds were established, I would like to have you send to the trustees of each board a copy of your letter to me and of this letter to you, so that it may be clear to them and to their successors that no act of mine in establishing these separate boards should ever be construed as indicative of my wish that they should always remain separate, or as a reason why the fullest and most complete cooperation or affiliation or absorption should not ultimately take place, if and when in the judgement of those responsible, such steps are deemed to be wise.

Affectionately
Your Father
John D. Rockefeller

26 Broadway
New York City

Ormond Beach
Florida
December 13, 1926

Dear Son:

Referring to our conversation, when at your house regarding high salaries, I would add that high though they are, as I expressed myself to you some years ago when the question was up, I still believe that the cost is less than by percentages, and there are practices in the percentage calculations that the administrators would not be tempted to follow in the case of a fixed salary.

Conditions here are all that heart could desire, and we are happy and contented and grateful, and looking with keenest interest for everything that pertains to the well-being of each one of you at home.

Remember the latch-string is out all the time.

With tenderest affection,
Father

26 Broadway
New York

---

26 Broadway
New York
December 16, 1926

Dear Father:

Your letter of the 13th is received. I am glad to have this further reflection of yours on the question of compensation for the higher officials of the various companies. It is undoubtedly true that a fixed salary, even if high, would be less costly to a company than a salary and bonus, the latter being based on the earnings. I am not sure, however, that the total paid in compensation in the latter plan would be larger in proportion to the total earnings of the company. Unless a percentage basis stimulates to increased earnings for the stockholders, it would not increase the compensation of the officer.

I am enclosing a clipping from a recent issue of the Wall Street Journal, which is very interesting and kindly. I am sure you will enjoy it.

I telegraphed you last night that David, Miss Scales and Mr. Gockler were leaving tomorrow (Friday) on the noon train for Ormond. The cold which David had at Thanksgiving time and from which he seemed to have recovered, has returned during the past week in the form of an irritating bronchial cough, which has finally made it unwise for him to continue in school these last days before vacation. He is up and about, not contagious or incapacitated, but simply constantly disturbed by the cough. A change of climate seems to be the thing that will most quickly rid him of this condition. I have therefore telegraphed you about arranging for room at the hotel for Miss Scales and Mr. Gockler. Mr. Gockler will be with David outside, and Miss Scales goes simply that there may be no responsibility on either you or Mrs. Evans for his welfare. David is perfectly delighted with the idea of being in Ormond for the vacation, and is eagerly looking forward to his arrival. Please do not have him or the others at all on your mind, for that would make Abby and me unhappy.

As you know, Mr. Cary is retiring at the end of the year. He has been with us many, many years. I have thought that it would be a nice thing for you and me to give him a gold watch. This I am sure he would appreciate enormously. Does the suggestion appeal to you? If so I will go ahead with it.

Affectionately
John

Ormond Beach, Florida

Florence M. Scales was the nurse-governess for David Rockefeller. Mr. Gockler was his tutor.

---

26 Broadway
New York
May 23, 1927

Dear Father:

Abby and I have just returned today from Atlanta, having had a most delightful time. We arrived at Atlanta late Wednesday afternoon. Mr. Arnett, formerly comptroller of the University of Chicago, who is now associated with us, is the President of the Spelman Board and went down with us to attend a board meeting. Young William Travers Jerome, son of the former District Attorney of New York City, a fine young fellow, who married one of Mr. Colgate's daughters, is also a member of the Spelman Board, and went down with us. That evening Major

Quinn, a leading Atlanta citizen and Vice-Chairman of the Spelman Board, gave a dinner for the Spelman Trustees and ourselves at one of Atlanta's country clubs. About forty were present including the leading citizens. It was a most delightful affair, and the interest thus expressed and aroused in Spelman was most helpful. Next morning we visited the college and saw the Sisters Chapel, which is in every way beautiful and satisfactory. I am enclosing a dinner card, of the dinner just referred to, which shows the facade of the chapel and the interior.

You will never know Spelman—it is so changed. It has now a most attractive campus with fine buildings, simple but well adapted to their purposes. We looked over the various buildings, met the school assembled in the chapel, had a few speeches and then were entertained at luncheon by the Economic Department students, who prepared the luncheon themselves. That afternoon the wife of the Governor of Georgia asked a few friends to meet us at tea. The dedication exercises took place in the chapel that evening. I am enclosing a program. The chapel was filled with white and colored people. It seats about twelve hundred. The great windows on either side were open, for the night was warm and beautiful, and each window was filled with an ocean of colored faces, eagerly looking in and listening. Hundreds, if not thousands, were turned away. Although the program was long the audience was interested and most appreciative. It was a real experience and in every way highly gratifying.

The next day at noon we left Atlanta, reaching Richmond Saturday morning and spending Saturday and Sunday at the College of William and Mary at Williamsburg, where we had a quiet and restful time. The trip was enjoyable and worth while from every point of view. Miss Tapley read your letter at the dedicatory exercises and spoke with deep appreciation of your uniform kindness and consideration.

This week we have the philanthropic boards meetings. A meeting of the General Education Board is to be held at the Princeton Inn on Thursday and Friday. I shall return to Pocantico Friday night and be there until Monday or Tuesday morning, since Monday is Memorial Day. I am hoping that it may be in your program to spend the weekend at Pocantico.

Young Mr. Donnell called on me this morning and spoke with such appreciation of his recent visit to you.

Affectionately,
John

Lakewood, N.J.

---

26 Broadway
New York
May 1, 1928

Dear Father:

We have had a pretty strenuous week, with matters at home in connection with the arrival of Bab's little daughter, and also with business matters. The chief problem in connection with the latter has been the question of the resignation of Colonel Stewart, which, in view of his recent testimony in Washington, it has seemed necessary to bring about. As you can well imagine, this is a serious situation and fraught with many difficulties and dangers. On the other hand, after long, exhaustive conferences, our office group here is unanimously of the opinion that no other course is open.

I have already had a full and satisfactory talk with Mr. Seubert, President of the company, and have the fullest assurance of his complete loyalty to the interests of the company.

This is just by way of information. I am leaving today for Seal Harbor, and hope to have a good rest for the balance of the week. Bab's baby is darling, and we are all devoted to her. Bab was a perfect trump throughout and has followed worthily in the footsteps of her mother. We are all proud of her.

I find on inquiry that our heating at No. 10 is by steam and not hot water, as I wrote you.

Looking forward to seeing you before long, and suggesting

that you destroy this letter, which is merely gossip in its content, I am,

Affectionately,
John

Lakewood, N.J.

Colonel Robert W. Stewart was the highly successful chairman of the Standard Oil Company of Indiana. In 1921, he and other oil men engaged in the purchase and sale of oil from and to their respective companies, which produced questionable personal profits. The transactions were uncovered during the Senate investigation of the Teapot Dome and Elk Hills oil reservations, which began in 1922. By 1928 the trail had led to Colonel Stewart. He, Junior, and others were called to testify before the Senate committee. Rockefeller was unwilling to accept Stewart's account of the transactions and asked Stewart to resign as chairman of the company. Stewart refused and Rockefeller mounted a well-publicized and successful proxy fight to force Stewart out.

Abby Milton, the daughter of Abby Rockefeller Milton and David M. Milton, was born on April 27, 1928.

---

26 Broadway
New York
May 23, 1928

Dear Father:

Your beautiful letter of May 22 is deeply appreciated and is most heartening. I am sure your message to Margaret will come as a balm to her poor sad heart.

We have been overwhelmed with grief at the death of Dr. Noguchi, the great Japanese scientist of the Rockefeller Institute staff, who, as you have read in the papers, died in South Africa, where he went to study yellow fever. Equally sad has been the death of Mr. James C. Colgate's youngest daughter within the last day or two. She was a beautiful young girl, just out of Vassar, who was to have been married last week and who died of pneumonia. How grateful we are that our dear ones are spared to us.

Last night all of the trustees of the four philanthropic boards, with the exception of three—two of whom were abroad, the third being Mr. Gates, who did not feel able to undergo the fatigue incident thereto—dined with me at our house. There were thirty of us at the dinner. The purpose of the gathering was to receive the report of the Interboard Committee, which has been at work for over a year on plans for reorganization and consolidation. The report of the Committee, which I have discussed with you from time to time and with which you have been in fullest accord, was, after full and valuable discussion, unanimously adopted. Mr. Fosdick, the chairman of the Committee, has been very able and indefatigable in his study of this vexed question, and presented his case in a masterly way last night. I feel that this is a very important step in progress in our philanthropic boards, and that the results that will ultimately be worked out in unification of the organizations will be a great improvement over the methods now in use. Today we had a meeting of the Rockefeller Foundation and tomorrow and the next day follow meetings of the other boards.

We are expecting to be at Tarrytown Friday night, remaining until Sunday night or Monday morning of this present weekend. If the weather takes a turn for the better and you are tempted to come up for the weekend, it will be a delight to see you. Several neighborhood friends are dining with us this Friday evening.

Bab and the baby are doing splendidly. They are moving to their house at Pocantico the end of next week.

On Sunday night Colonel Lindbergh took a family supper with us. John and Nelson were at home, Bab and Dave were down, so that the whole family was together. We found him a simple, unostentatious, cleancut, charming fellow and thoroughly enjoyed the intimate visit with him. We have asked him to spend the coming weekend with us in the country, which he expressed a desire to do if it is possible. As yet we have not heard whether it will be possible.

Affectionately,
John

Lakewood, N.J.

---

26 Broadway
New York
June 8, 1928

Dear Father:

Abby and I got back this morning from Nashville. We had a delightful time and a really good rest, for we were on the train each way about thirty hours. Our experience at Fisk University, which is one of the leading colored universities of the country, was most interesting and gratifying. We came back in the private car of Mr. Paul Cravath, the lawyer, whose father was the founder of Fisk University and who has himself been the president of the board of trustees for the last twenty-five years. The Chamber of Commerce of Nashville gave us a reception the night we left. Everyone was most kind, and we felt well repaid for having gone.

I am hoping that you are beginning to think of moving to Pocantico, for we shall be there weekends right along and frequently between, from now on, with the exception of our proposed trip up the lakes, on which we leave Monday, June 25th, to be gone about ten days.

Affectionately
John

Lakewood, N.J.

Lakewood, N.J.
June 8th, 1928

Dear Son:

We have read your Nashville speech and are perfectly delighted with it. We think it one of the best, if not the best, you have made at any time. It has the right ring, and we feel certain it will do much good.

All goes well with us here. We are happy and contented and leading a quiet and peaceful life.

With tenderest affection,
Father

Telephone message to 26 Broadway
New York

Junior gave the commencement address at Fisk University in 1928. He later reworked the speech into his address for the USO in 1942 in which he set forth his personal Credo.

---

26 Broadway
New York
June 14, 1928

Dear Father:

As your birthday approaches, I am wishing, as I always do at these anniversary seasons, that there was something you really wanted that I could give you. The fur coat, one of my early attempts, was not wholly successful from your point of view although eminently so from mine, for I continue to enjoy it each winter and to be grateful to you for returning it to me.

It took a long time to bring you to the point where you were willing to accept the Crane car, but when finally won over, you were so broad minded as to be willing to let me repeat the dose and get you a second car, which gave me the greatest pleasure. Although I think the Crane is still a wonderful car, it is becoming somewhat antiquated. My family is rebelling against the continued use of ours, so much so that there was a mutiny last year, with the result that we bought a Rolls Royce and a Lincoln, both of which have given great satisfaction.

If you would be willing to have me take either one or both of your Crane-Simplexes off your hands, in the event that you are through with them, and replace them, one or both, with a Rolls Royce or a Lincoln or one of each, or a car of any other make that you prefer, I should be perfectly delighted and would get quite as much pleasure out of the transaction as you possibly could from the subsequent use of the cars.

Please give the suggestion thought at your leisure, and if it appeals to you I shall be more than happy to act upon it. If it does not, I shall quite understand, for I feel with you that to receive gifts that one neither needs or cares for is an embarrassment rather than a pleasure.

Affectionately,
John

Lakewood, N.J.

Golf House
Lakewood, N.J.
June 19, 1928

Dear Son:

It goes without saying that I deeply appreciate your beautiful letter of the 14th, with the suggestion of a present for me on the occasion of my birthday.

Your presence, and that of the other dear ones of our family, is all that I desire. I would tell you frankly if I could think of anything else in the world I would like to have. In truth, I do not. I am happy and contented, and if at any time I can make a suggestion as to something that it would give you pleasure to present to me, I will not hesitate to tell you.

Please do not mistake me. I am truly appreciative. My cup is full and running over, and my days are filled with brightness and cheer. I have all that heart could wish, and many times more than I could ever deserve. I am grateful that I have my faculties, and I have due appreciation of all those things, which make the blessings of life so much sweeter.

With tenderest affection,
Father

26 Broadway
New York

Kijkuit
Pocantico Hills, N.Y.
September 1, 1928

Dear Son:

Thank you for your beautiful letter of the 27th.

I sincerely feel that we can accomplish all that we desire by carefully co-operating and conferring as to ways and means, resisting the temptation to take on new obligations, not only, but gradually eliminating many of the old, thus reducing the volume of matters requiring attention, and with the incoming of the boys to begin to assume some of the responsibilities that we have carried, this, I am sure, will afford great promise of comfort and relief.

Everything is going on well here, and you must get all the benefit possible in the remaining days before returning home, and when you do return, under no circumstances should you plunge into work without resolving carefully to observe all limitations. If more responsibility presents itself I know there are a number round about you who are only too eager to do all in their power to help, and to avail of this will prove of great benefit all around.

We are enjoying perfect weather today, and seem to be through with the heated term, for the present.

With tenderest affection,
Father

26 Broadway
New York

Ormond Beach
Florida
February 15, 1929

Dear Son:

Until receipt of your message of the 13th, I seemed to be possessed with the thought that we were not to write letters, and I do not feel at all certain that this will reach you. Your good letter of January 9th came duly to hand, and we were delighted to hear that you were all in good health and enjoying your trip. The days have gone very rapidly, and we are beginning to look forward to going to Lakewood about the first of April. The weather has been excellent, and we have all been in good condition of health and have enjoyed our stay here.

I presume you have been kept fully posted on the affairs of the office so far as you have desired to hear of them. We have had our usual run of visitors, and are now expecting Dr. Vincent, who will come next week, and possibly Mrs. Warner. You very likely have had a detailed account of the death of Mr. Gates and the serious condition of Mrs. Gates, and the daughter, and one of the grandchildren. It seems a fearful calamity. On receipt of word of Mr. Gates' death I sent the following message to Mrs. Gates:

"I am deeply shocked and saddened to learn of the passing of your dear husband, my companion, friend and invaluable helper for the long, long years in our business and philanthropic undertakings. Too much cannot be said of his most helpful service in these relations. He will be greatly missed by the multitudes whose lives have been blessed as a result of the beneficent influences in which his labors in connection with those of others of our associates have done so much toward uplifting our fellow men and in relieving world-wide suffering. Those of us who remain unite in paying highest tribute to his beloved memory. Be assured of my sympathy for you and each of your dear ones in this sad bereavement."

Our home here is more pleasant than ever, and we are contented and happy, and are constantly saying how much we have to be grateful for. We receive on every hand, commendations, too many to enumerate, of your course in the Indiana matter, and we keep closely in touch. Indeed, yesterday we sent four long messages and they seemed to be very acceptable to the committee. I presume you have had from the office a little published response from me which seemed necessary a few days ago, and which appears to have been well received, and we hope may do some good.

We trust you are all getting the needful rest, and that you have succeeded well in dismissing all thoughts that would in any wise interfere with this object. Our friends here are more than ever kind and helpful to us, and it is most reassuring and cheering, and so we keep saying, gratitude, gratitude, gratitude.

Do not hurry back. The world will wag along, and now that you are so far away, you may have occasion to regret if you do not take in to the full all the favoring opportunities afforded for enjoyment and entertainment.

With tenderest affection,
Father

To be forwarded by New York office

Junior, Abby, their son David, Dr. James H. Breasted of the University of Chicago, and some other friends visited Egypt, Palestine, and

France on an extended trip in the spring of 1929. George E. Vincent was president of the Rockefeller Foundation from 1917–1929.

Golf House
Lakewood, N.J.
June 12, 1929

Dear Son:

Answering yours of the 10th, I am deeply touched by and grateful for your suggestion to make me a birthday present of a Rolls-Royce, but my dear son, I could not conscientiously allow myself to be possessed of any more cars until we have fewer on hand which are entirely satisfactory for our service. I dare not allow such an example to go out with my endorsement before all of our young people coming along, and our neighbors and others.

I am most grateful to say that I am happy and perfectly contented with the cars we now have. The greatest birthday gift that can possibly be bestowed upon me is the presence of my dear ones and their affection, and under your leadership they are a constant delight and satisfaction to me.

Please understand that this is from no lack of most keen appreciation of your kind offer.

With tenderest affection,
Father

26 Broadway
New York

Golf House
Lakewood, N.J.
June 13, 1929

Dear Son:

After reflection in the night, last night, I am emboldened to say, respecting your kind offer of the Rolls-Royce in yours of the 10th, and my answer of yesterday, that if it would be your pleasure to give me this value in cash, in place of the car, I would be glad to make judicious use of it in connection with my most needy charity cases, thus making the investment of the greatest value to us both.

This is only a suggestion, and you must exercise your own good judgement, with which, be assured, I shall be perfectly satisfied.

With tenderest affection,
Father

26 Broadway
New York

---

26 Broadway
New York
July 5, 1929

Dear Father:

In line with our recent correspondence, I am happy to enclose herewith, as a present on your ninetieth birthday, my check for $19,000, being the cost of a Rolls Royce car which I offered you, and instead of which you said you would prefer to have cash.

What a wonderful thing it is—not only to have lived ninety years, but to have lived so usefully, so constructively and so happily for that length of time. Usually anyone of that age is marking time. With you, it is wholly different. You are daily making contributions large and small, of one kind of another, to make the world better, to make individuals happier and to bring strength and sunshine and joy into the lives of all those who come in contact with you.

We are grateful beyond expression for your splendid health and for all those qualities of head and heart which continue, as through the long years past, to make us love you, admire you and want to be like you.

Affectionately,
John

Pocantico Hills, N.Y.

---

26 Broadway
New York
December 19, 1929

Dear Father:

I am sorry not to be sending you a Christmas present of more value than the two dozen golf balls and the several fountain pens which are going forward to you and which I hope may be useful.

On the other hand, you know what a wealth of love and affection is directed toward you from me, not only at the Christmas season, but during every one of the three hundred and sixty-five days of each year.

John's coming into the office brings back vividly to mind my early days of association with you, and the great joy and inspiration into which that association has developed as the years have gone by. I marvel as I review in memory your unfailing kindness, consideration and forbearance with me, and am grateful beyond expression for all that you have been to me during these many years, not to mention the wonderful gifts that you have given me, which beggar description.

In the hope that the approaching Christmas may be the happiest of your life, and that the New Year may bring you continued health, peace and joy, I am,

Affectionately,
John

Ormond Beach, Florida

Ormond Beach
Florida
December 24, 1929

Dear Son:

I am just in receipt of your inexpressibly beautiful letter of the 19th. The presents are all that heart could wish, and the long, happy years since you came, as John is now coming, have brought me the greatest joy and satisfaction, and invaluable help, the appreciation of which I have no words to express. You have far exceeded my expectations, and now that John has come, and the others will be coming, please renew your diligence to drop off, as rapidly as possible, the cares and responsibilities which in the nature of the case have borne so heavily upon you these many years.

In doing this you will best fit the boys for service and save yourself from the effects of too long a strain of overwork. I rejoice every time I hear that you are delegating responsibility to others, and you will find this the wisest and best course to pursue.

We are having a lovely time with the boys. The weather is

cold, but we are all cheery and well, and all unite in loving greetings to the rest of you in the North.

With tenderest affection,
Father

26 Broadway
New York

Ormond Beach
Florida
March 14, 1930

Dear Father:

I spoke of your wedding present to Nelson and Mary the other day, since you not infrequently ask for suggestions in such matters. I thought you would want to know that you gave Bab $20,000 in securities. I presume you will not think to do differently with Nelson and Mary. Since the wedding present usually goes to the bride, but since it is Nelson who is your grandchild, I was wondering what you would think of dividing the gift, $10,000 to Mary and $10,000 to Nelson. If there were some special gift which Mary would like, such as jewelry, or which both might need, such as furniture, that might wisely be considered. We have, however, given and are giving Mary jewelry and shall probably furnish any apartment or house which the young couple may occupy, so that these needs will not exist. $10,000 to each of the young people would, I am sure, be greatly appreciated, and I feel confident they would both lay the sum away in some safe investment as a nest-egg.

This is of course merely a suggestion, and this note needs no acknowledgement.

Affectionately,
John

Ormond Beach, Florida

Nelson A. Rockefeller married Mary Todhunter Clark on June 23, 1930.

---

26 Broadway
New York
May 16, 1930

Dear Father:

Thank you for your beautiful telegram. I am striving to follow the good advice which it contains, but life is so interesting that it is difficult to keep as free and as restful as I know I should.

I regret to say that Dr. Allen's Institute of Public Service has secured a contribution from some interested friend which enables it to publish the history of your life which Dr. Allen has written and of which I spoke when at Lakewood the other week. We are told the book will be on sale on Saturday of this week. The book is not written from a sensational and catchy point of view, as was the Winkler biography. It is more a philosophical or psycho-analytical study of your life. I think, therefore, that its sale will be exceedingly limited and that it will attract very little attention. While I of course regret its publication, I do not believe any great harm or annoyance will be caused thereby.

Affectionately,
John

Lakewood, N.J.

William H. Allen, Rockefeller: Giant, Dwarf, Symbol *(New York, 1930); John K. Winkler,* John D. Rockefeller: A Portrait In Oils *(Cornwall, N.Y.: Blue Ribbon Books, Cornwall Press. 1929).*

---

26 Broadway
New York
June 3, 1930

Dear Father:

At the time the several boards sold their holdings of stock in the Prairie Oil and Gas Company and the Prairie Pipeline Company, I was desirous of selling my holdings in these two companies also. However, out of deference to your view I gladly retained the stock and said I would continue to hold it.

The matter of the sale of these two stocks is again up. Mr. Cutler has been discussing it with you. You know all the factors in the situation. I feel more than ever that it is wise to dispose of these stocks. Through Mr. Cutler, you have kindly released me from my engagement to hold them longer, and have said you would not oppose my selling them if I so desire. This I much appreciate and thank you for. I have authorized Mr. Cutler to sell my holdings for the total price which I could have gotten had I sold them in 1928 when the boards sold.

Mr. Cutler tells me you are not at the moment inclined to sell your own stock in these companies. May I venture to urge that you seriously consider so doing, for the following reasons:

1. The Prairie Oil & Gas Company is to become more or less a Sinclair company, which will indirectly if not directly control

the Prairie Pipeline Company. Sinclair will be an active and dominating factor in it. I cannot but feel that any stock-holding support of him would be apt to lead to public misunderstanding and misinterpretation and that it would also raise questions in the minds of the management of the Standard Oil Companies as to how sincere we were in deposing Colonel Stewart, who was intimately associated with Sinclair in various transactions.

2. Fitzpatrick is, I am told, slated for the position of chairman of the Board of the enlarged Prairie-Sinclair Company. While your estimate of Fitzpatrick may be right, Mr. Debevoise, Mr. Cutler and I have never had the confidence in him which you have; in fact we do not entirely trust him and would be very glad not to have our office through either your or my stock ownership even indirectly responsible for his management.

3. All of the oil men with whom we have talked, without a single exception, have strongly advised our withdrawing from the Prairie Company. They clearly believe that the Prairie will have a hard row to hoe in the future, and it is also quite evident that the plans which various of them have for their own development may more than likely seriously affect the future business of the Prairie.

May I say in closing that I shall feel a sense of great personal relief when neither you nor I nor any of our interests are stockholders in either the Prairie Oil or the Prairie Pipeline Companies.

Affectionately,
John

Lakewood, N.J.

W. S. Fitzpatrick was chairman of the Prairie Oil and Gas Company. He provided testimony in the Teapot Dome investigation which led to the disclosure of Colonel Robert Stewart's activities. Thomas M. Debevoise was the last in a series of in-house counsels for Senior and Junior. He was a fraternity brother of Junior's at Brown and entered the office in 1925.

Golf House
Lakewood, N.J.
June 4, 1930

Dear Son:

Answering yours of the 3rd, I have carefully weighed your points, and appreciate them, and will keep them all in mind. I am entirely willing for you to do whatever you think best about selling your interests, and in case your offer is accepted I shall want to weigh the subject carefully with reference to mine before deciding not to sell, but should I retain mine, as I have contemplated (in more or less of a temporary way) I hope and believe that I shall proceed in such manner as shall in no wise be hurtful to our general and common interests, from all points of view.

Affectionately,
Father

26 Broadway
New York

Plaza-Athenee
Paris, France
November 13, 1930

Dear Father:

We are in Paris again, having returned last night from a three-weeks motor trip which took us into Northern Spain for a part of the time and through Southern France and the Pyrenees Mountains the balance of the time. We had one of the chauffeurs we have had frequently before over here and who is an excellent driver and an equally good courier and guide. The entire trip was made in the car. William, my man, went with us and we took on top of the car all the baggage needed. We were greatly interested in Spain and had hoped to visit the Southern portion as well. Sightseeing, however, proved rather strenuous so that we decided to content ourselves with seeing the northern portion of the country more at our leisure and thus enable us to spend a few days restfully by the seashore in Biarritz, in Southern France, and in the Pyrenees Mountains nearby. We shall be here in Paris for a few days to enable Abby to finish certain shopping that she has on hand, and sail next Wednesday, reaching New York the day before Thanksgiving.

There has been a great deal of rain in Europe this year. The rivers of France have been flooded almost to the danger point. We wished that some of the surplus water might be falling in the United States where it is so much needed. The children write that the Fall has been beautiful in Pocantico, and David especially seems to have greatly enjoyed being there. They all speak of you from time to time and of their pleasure in being with you.

Thank you for your several telegrams which were most welcome. We had letters and frequently cables from Nelson and Mary who are now in Hong Kong, China. They are having a marvelous time and are enthusiastic over all they see.

Looking forward greatly to seeing you on Thanksgiving Day, I am,

Affectionately,
John

Lakewood, N.J.

---

26 Broadway
New York
December 15, 1930

Dear Father:

I have been very remiss in not having thanked you earlier for your letter of December 1st with the interesting clippings in connection with your arrival in the South, and particularly for the copy of your beautiful letter of December 1st to Mr. Gore, Editor of the Deland Sun-News. Since I know that your reception by reporters in the South has sometimes been disturbing and annoying, I am the more gratified at the change of front evidenced by the article which you enclose and by others I have seen. Thank you for sharing this article with me.

All goes well with us here. We spent Friday night and Saturday in the country each week since you left and have had very good weather there. The boys are continuing to enjoy horseback riding on the new roads and paths and Abby and I have had a number of good drives.

I am going to Boston tonight to make one of my regular visits to the oculist there, and also to see a business man from Maine. I shall get home tomorrow afternoon.

We are loving the new Riverside Church. The services there are gratifying, stimulating and uplifting in the highest degree. Dr. Gilkey of the University of Chicago Chapel preached there yesterday. The main floor of the auditorium was practically filled.

Margaret has not been very well lately and has had an X-ray taken at the Institute. This seems to indicate that she has some form of rheumatism, which may account for some of her discomfort. Abby is working with her to get just the right doctor and treatment.

I must not forget to tell you that a week ago Sunday at the communion service in the afternoon, Abby brought her letter from the Briarcliff Church and was received into the membership of the Riverside Church. There were received at the same time 187 persons, which represents the new membership of the last three months, nearly one hundred having been received in the early fall. These people are fine people, professors, educators, writers and throughout of the intelligent and thoughtful class.

Affectionately,
John

Ormond Beach, Florida

Margaret Strong de Cuevas, born in 1897, was the daughter of Bessie Rockefeller Strong, Senior's eldest daughter.

John D. Rockefeller, Jr., and Abby Aldrich Rockefeller, 1901.

John D. Rockefeller, 1884.

John D. Rockefeller, painting by John Singer Sargent, Ormond Beach, Florida, February 1917.

John D. Rockefeller, Jr., 1905.

John D. Rockefeller, Jr., December 1940.

Residence of John D. Rockefeller, 997 Euclid Avenue, Cleveland, Ohio. Purchased in 1868; demolished in 1938.

"Golf House," residence of John D. Rockefeller at Lakewood, New Jersey. Purchased in 1901; demolished in 1960.

"The Casements," residence of John D. Rockefeller at Ormond Beach, Florida. Purchased in 1918; on the National Registry of Historic Places; now a civic and cultural center for the town of Ormond Beach.

"Kykuit," residence of John D. Rockefeller, John D. Rockefeller, Jr., and Nelson A. Rockefeller, Pocantico Hills, New York. Property purchased in 1893; original house on site burned in 1904; present house completed in 1911. Now owned by the National Trust for Historic Preservation.

"Abeyton Lodge," residence of John D. Rockefeller, Jr., at Pocantico Hills, New York. Occupied by the family from 1904 to 1937; demolished in 1938.

"The Eyrie," residence of John D. Rockefeller, Jr., at Seal Harbor, Maine. Purchased in 1910; demolished in 1962.

JOHN D. ROCKEFELLER

Ormond Beach, Feb. 6, 1919.

Dear Son:

I am giving you 50,000 shares of the stock of the Standard Oil Company of New Jersey. I have written Mr. Cary to deliver the same to you.

Affectionately,

John D. Rockefeller.

Mr. John D. Rockefeller, Jr.,
26 Broadway, New York.

JOHN D. ROCKEFELLER

Ormond Beach, Fla.,
December 27, 1919.

Dear Son:

I thank you for the beautiful and most acceptable Christmas gifts - I might say, too numerous to mention; and to cap the climax, the lovely visit from you and Babbie.

Affectionately,

Father

26 Broadway
New York

Miss Gilbert

February 3, 1933

Dear Father:

There came to you on December 29th a letter from a Miss Alice H. Gilbert enclosing a number of letters written by Mother and Aunt Lute when they were girls to a Mrs. Hawley, the grandmother of Miss Gilbert, who taught music in Burlington, Iowa, and among whose pupils were mother and Aunt Lute. There must be twenty of these letters. I have only had a chance to glance at them so far. They are most interesting and it is fine to have them.

I have written Miss Gilbert a letter of thanks on your behalf and shall bring the letters to Ormond when I come down. This note I am sending merely so that you will know about the matter in case a further letter from Miss Gilbert should come to you. In that event perhaps Mr. Davis will pass the letter on to me for such answer as may seem necessary.

Affectionately,

John.

Mr. John D.Rockefeller
The Casements
Ormond Beach, Florida

Ormond Beach
Florida
December 23, 1930

Dear Son:

I am just in receipt of yours of the 20th.

I deeply appreciate the gift of the beautiful ties, but far more deeply the loyal devotion and affectionate regard of my dear son.

With all the best wishes of the glad holiday time, and with tenderest affection.

Father

26 Broadway
New York

---

26 Broadway
New York
December 29, 1930

Dear Father:

In looking over some of the reports of the Boards, I am moved to send you the following facts:

In June of this year the General Education Board sold securities valued on the ledger at $20,000,000, for which there was received $40,000,000. In other words, there was an increase in value of that portion of your gift to the General Education Board of $20,000,000. Again the General Education Board has appropriated since its organization $214,000,000, of which appropriations $174,000,000 have been paid to date, leaving practically $40,000,000 still to the paid. Of the total appropriated $182,000,000 was for educational work among whites and $26,000,000 for educational work among colored people.

Again, the Rockefeller Institute has now in round figures an endowment of something over $60,000,000, in addition to $10,000,000 invested in land and buildings.

These facts and figures are very moving to me, and I am sure will be interesting to you.

Affectionately,
John

Ormond Beach, Florida

---

26 Broadway
New York
January 5, 1931

Dear Father:

Over a month ago you sent word to us that you had a fur robe at Pocantico which you no longer used and which we might have if we so desired. It has proved to be the beautiful robe made of fox skins which, I think, Ezekiel Davidson once brought you from South Africa. It has not only the skins, but the fox tails as well, all hanging from the robe in a most gay and ornamental fashion. We are having the robe lined for a motor robe, and are perfectly delighted with it. It is a very beautiful and unusual collection of skins, and will make a stunning lap robe. Abby and I thank you a thousand times for this gift, which bids fair to be as acceptable as the fur coat you once returned to me.

Affectionately
John

Ormond Beach, Florida

---

26 Broadway
New York
January 27, 1931

Dear Father:

I have pledged $250,000 to the New York quota of the Ten Million Dollar Campaign of the American Red Cross for funds for national relief. Tarrytown is seeking to raise $3,000, its quota. It occurs to me that our proportion of that amount, having in mind our interests at Tarrytown, would be about $500. I am wondering whether you would not be disposed to make this contribution yourself.

Affectionately,
John

Ormond Beach, Florida

John D. Rockefeller, Sr. agreed to give $500 toward the Tarrytown Red Cross drive.

Arizona Inn
Tucson, Arizona
March 6, 1931

Dear Father:-

We have been here a week tonight and have had practically continuous sunshine. We are most comfortably and delightfully situated in our little family hotel, all so new and fresh, and are as quiet and detached as we could wish.

The other day in the lunch room at the hotel a lady sitting at a nearby table bowed to me. I bowed back but without recognizing her. Later I was informed she was Ida Tarbell, who is staying almost next door to us here.

We have an automobile by the week, ride horseback and sit out in the sun. The desert in which Tucson is located is perhaps twenty to thirty miles long and the same in width; the mountains surrounding it on every side.

We sleep nine or ten hours a night and are being as lazy and restful as possible. Abby's cold is entirely gone and she is looking and feeling very well, as am I also.

The memories of our happy two weeks with you are still bright and fragrant. How good you were to us. We enjoyed each moment of our stay.

Affectionately,
John

Lakewood, N.J.

---

26 Broadway
New York
June 8, 1931

Dear Father:

For many years you were a contributor to the Northfield School at Mt. Hermon, founded by Dwight L. Moody, the great evangelist. You have contributed to both the building funds in the past and also for some years towards expenses. No recent contribution has been made.

June 12th of this year is the fiftieth anniversary of the founding of the school. An effort has been on foot for some months to raise a three million dollar fund in celebration of the anniversary. The fund is to be used as follows:

$300,000—Increase of Faculty Salaries, a total of $15,000 per year.
500,000—Teachers' Retirement Plan.
200,000—Imperative repairs and remodeling of oldest buildings.
2,000,000—General Endowment.

All but $314,000 of the $3,000,000 has been raised. You are asked to contribute this sum or any part of it.

Because of what Mr. Moody stood for, because of your deep interest in him and your support of this work in years gone by, I am laying the matter before you. If you are inclined to make a contribution but hesitate to contribute to endowment, you could request that your gift should apply on the $500,000 needed for Teachers' Retirement Plan or partly for that and partly for the $200,000 needed for the renovation of buildings.

Affectionately,
John

Lakewood, N.J.

Lakewood, N.J.
June 10, 1931

Dear Son:

Your letter of the 8th just received in regard to a contribution for the Northfield Schools. I exceedingly regret not to join in this undertaking. I wish I could feel that I could do so without its taking the place of some things that I want to be sure to get out of the way first.

Affectionately,
Father

26 Broadway
New York

The Eyrie
Seal Harbor, Maine
August 18, 1931

Dear Father:

It hardly seems possible that I have been back here a week tomorrow. I recall our visit together at Pocantico with the greatest pleasure, and am still saying to myself, is there another father who would have taken the trouble to move from one house to another just for the sake of being with his son?

We have had a good deal of fog here since my return, but today is bright and pleasant. Ned Ballard and Bessie have motored to Maine and are spending a day or two at a nearby hotel. They are to drive with us this morning. John is motoring up and arrives this noon. Laurance is on the ocean and will be here shortly. The other boys are at home, except Nelson, who is back at Pocantico, as you know. We see Admiral Byrd every once in a while. He and his wife dined with us Saturday night, and our boys had a delightful time with them yesterday at their place.

What a wonderful trip you must have had back to Lakewood. Your early start enabled you to completely avoid the traffic. I am glad you had a chance to try the overhead speedway along the docks and the Holland Tube.

At my request, John was recently looking over our cars at Pocantico, to see what ones needed repairs, what could well be exchanged. His attention was called to Miss Payne's car, since we have none of that make. The men spoke well of the car as to its wearing qualities, and although it is four years old its appearance is good. They happened to mention to John that it was of a model which has very poor springs and rides exceedingly hard. Unless you are planning to trade it off within the year, as you probably will, John wondered whether it would not be worth while to put hydraulic shock absorbers on the car, which could be done for a very few dollars and would greatly improve the riding qualities of the car. This our own mechanics at Pocantico could do if you so desired, and John could easily see to it. Please pay no attention to this gratuitous suggestion of John's, unless it interests you. What boys do not see when it comes to cars it would be difficult to imagine.

Affectionately,
John

Lakewood, N.J.

---

26 Broadway
New York
September 23, 1931

Dear Father:

Thank you for your letter of September 12th, in which you have made certain observations regarding your own dairy at Lakewood, which you are thinking of giving up, and the recent sale by your old friend, Mr. Barnes, of Connecticut, of his dairy in Connecticut.

I suppose no one deludes himself into thinking that a private farm pays. It is obviously a luxury, like a yacht, although I hope not quite so great an extravagance. I have not myself great interest in farming, nor have I any knowledge of it. On the other hand, Abby and I have felt that a farm centre at Pocantico such as I have talked with you about and such as we have been planning to build, would be of interest to the children and would be another thing that would help to tie them to the place. Thus far we are fortunate in that both the married children are fond of Pocantico and desirous of living there permanently. The other children already talk as though they felt the same. I am developing and unifying the place having that in mind. It is a possibility which seems to me so desirable as to justify a good deal of time, trouble and expense to encourage it. As this possibility grows and the children increasingly take up their home life at Pocantico, I had thought the farm might be managed by a committee of the children, those of them particularly interested in that sort of thing. It would be rather in the interest and to the advantage of all who lived there; hence it would be a personal thing and one to which they would enjoy giving attention.

I do not doubt that generally speaking you are in agreement with me in regard to this matter, as I am of course in agreement with you on the point that one can buy one's farm products much cheaper than they can be produced, although perhaps with less satisfaction.

Affectionately,
John

Pocantico Hills, N.Y.

Junior did build a farm complex at Pocantico Hills. It consisted of stables, hay lofts, a cattle barn with silo, and supporting buildings. It operated as a farm until Junior died.

Ormond Beach
Florida
December 28, 1931

Dear Son:

Thank you for the beautiful shawl, the useful umbrella holder, the exquisite flowers and wreaths and the book descriptive of the Riverside church, which you kindly sent me—all most acceptable and greatly appreciated—as well as all the wonderful things you are doing for me from day to day the year around.

All goes well with us. We are busy indeed, and tonight is our Christmas celebration. We have had a number of seasonal gatherings, larger and smaller, and more of them than usual, to say nothing of the photographs, etc., all of which have brought pleasure, and, we hope a little good to somebody.

We built our first fire this morning in my room. The temperature was 60 outside.

It is taking unusual patience and wisdom for these days

through which we are passing and I hope the experiences will result in benefit to the multitudes, though they are not just what we should have chosen for a real pleasant time.

We are anxiously looking forward to the visit from you and Abby. Do be careful, both of you, and observe your limitations regardless of the clamor of the people, who would ride you to death. We must all stand up for our own protection, and down here we are trying every day to learn that lesson and counsel together as to the wisest means of accomplishing it with the least tax or friction, and with the utmost kindliness.

I am still rejoicing that I went to the New York osteopath, and we have one here in whom Mrs. Evans delights. He seems to be wonderful and she has had him ten or twelve times with gratifying results. We will save him up for you and Abby.

With tenderest affection for each and every one of you
Father

26 Broadway
New York

---

26 Broadway
New York
April 12, 1932

Dear Father:

I am greatly interested in what you say about the improvements you are making at Ormond, particularly in the wonderful apartment which Abby and I occupy. A door from the little sun room to the veranda sounds quite exciting. We are still regretting not having been able to go to Ormond as planned and as we had so eagerly anticipated doing. The boys' vacations end this Friday. You will be coming North shortly and it is pretty late to go so far South. Abby and I have not had any let-up this winter, and are therefore planning to slip down to the Virginia Hot Springs on Friday for a few days—not longer.

We are all well except that David was in bed with a bad cold most of last week. My unsympathetic view is that the many parties he attended the week before during his vacation were the cause of his undoing. Of course David does not agree with this theory nor does his more indulgent mother. Nevertheless, whatever the cause was, he has lost four days out of the first week of school after vacation. Let us hope that the memories of the good times he had during the vacations have compensated him.

Last Wednesday night I gave a dinner to about two dozen business leaders. It was Mr. Debevoise's suggestion that a dinner should be given in honor of Mr. Wiggin, thinking that it would help to allay the rumors that were rife earlier in the year in regard to our not backing Mr. Wiggin and there being some split between him and Winthrop. About a dozen of his directors were among the guests, including Mr. Debevoise and Mr. Cutler, Bert Milbank, and Mr. Ecker, and in addition Mr. Morgan came, Mr. Teagle, Mr. Taylor, the head of the Steel Company, Mr. Owen Young, Mr. Brisbane, Mr. Wooley, head of the Radiator Company, whose young vice-president, Turck, came down to visit you with Nelson, and two or three others including, much to my satisfaction, John and Nelson. The evening was very pleasantly spent and Mr. Debevoise seemed to feel that what he had in mind had been well accomplished. I wish you might have been there to have met the gentlemen.

We have been doing over the Saportas house for Bab and Dave this summer. It is going to be most attractive and the young people are enthusiastic about it.

Looking forward to seeing you in Lakewood before many weeks, I am,

Affectionately,
John

Ormond Beach, Florida

Albert Wiggin was chairman of the Governing Council of the Chase

National Bank after its merger with the Equitable Trust Company in 1930. The Rockefellers owned about 4% of the stock of the merged company. Winthrop W. Aldrich, Junior's brother-in-law, a board member of the Equitable, was president of the new corporation.

About six months after this dinner, Wiggin retired. In 1933, the Pecora Senate committee, investigating the banking industry, led Wiggin to reveal that he had lent himself large sums of money, speculated in Chase stock, and engaged in other breaches of fiduciary trust.

Fenton Turck was associated with Nelson A. Rockefeller in a company, Special Works, which sought to find tenants for the new Rockefeller Center.

Ormond Beach
Florida
April 13, 1932

Dear Son:

Your letter of April 11th, with it enclosures, having to do with your purchase from me in 1922 of the Forest Hill estate, was duly received.

You are right in assuming that I did not, at the time, share your feeling as to the desirability of giving the whole or a portion of this property to the city for a public park. In the meantime the growth of the city around the place has made it still more doubtful as to whether the public interest would best be served were it to be ultimately set aside for a public park.

In selling the property to you I made no condition that it should be so used. I shall be entirely satisfied with whatever disposition of the property you finally decide it is wise to make, whether it be to devote it in whole or part to public purposes, park or otherwise, or dispose of it on a commercial basis or hold it.

Affectionately,
Father

26 Broadway
New York

---

26 Broadway
New York
November 15, 1932

Dear Father:

I have received with much appreciation your several splendid telegrams, one from Jacksonville, one on your arrival in Ormond and one since, and thank you for all of them.

After the rain of last week we have had a week of bright clear sunny days, which we have greatly enjoyed. Particularly grateful were we that the day of John's wedding was so beautiful. Everything went like clockwork. The great church was filled with the exception of the top gallery. I suppose at least fifteen hundred people, possibly more, all of them invited guests, witnessed the wedding, and what a beautiful wedding it was. The church, so stately in architecture, so inspiring in the beauty and richness of its carving and glass, was a fitting background for the pageant that took place that afternoon. The wedding party was truly magnificent. David and the usher who walked with him were the shortest of the twelve ushers. You can imagine what giants they were. The bridesmaids, dressed in deep red with the maid of honor in purple, were all of them slender and tall, while the bride and groom were worthy leaders of their splendid attendants. John was as calm, as self possessed, as dignified and as handsome as any man could be, and Blanchette worthy in every way of her part in the ceremony. Mrs. Warner and Miss Duncan sat beside us in the front seat. Most if not all of the people from our immediate office were at the church and I think practically our whole household, with many from the country. Everyone spoke with enthusiasm of the beauty and stateliness of the wedding. We were happy to see in practically all the papers the comment as to its simplicity. While the young people have been under a great strain in getting ready for the great day, they came through with flying colors in every way and did themselves proud. Spending the night in town, they sailed the next afternoon for Bermuda, where they will have a month of rest and quiet.

Now that this important event is over—an event which has brought to us all such great happiness, we are settling down into the regular routine of living again. On Thursday of this week occurs the dinner to Mr. Ballard in connection with which you wrote the letter to him. Friday night and all day Saturday our Foreign Mission survey group is holding a large meeting, to which some five hundred people have been invited representing the seven Missionary boards, with their officers, whose laymen have been back of the inquiry, as well as representatives of all the other missionary societies in this country. The report will be presented by the various members of the commission, and finally an opportunity to discuss its recommendations and decide what, if anything, shall be done about them will be given. We are looking forward with great interest to this gathering.

Since my letter to you of this morning it has been ascertained that the gentleman who was supposed to have been in Washington has been at his home ill all the time; the nature of the malady we do not yet know.

With warm remembrances to Mrs. Evans and Mrs. Mitchell, I am,

Affectionately,
John

Ormond Beach, Florida

John D. Rockefeller 3rd, married Blanchette Ferry Hooker on November 11, 1932.

Junior contributed $363,000 toward the Layman's Foreign Mission

Inquiry, which sent a study commission to China, Japan, and India in 1931. The Inquiry resulted in the publication in 1932 of Re-Thinking Missions. *The study influenced Junior's future religious giving.*

---

26 Broadway
New York
February 1, 1933

Dear Father:

I am borrowing some seven or eight million dollars. I have fairly extensive commitments coming due during this year which will considerably exceed my income, after deducting the very heavy income taxes due for last year.

As you know, I have a large amount of Government and State tax free bonds on which I could easily borrow many times the sum I shall need this year. While under normal conditions I would meet the situation that way, in view of the uncertainty of the future and of the many things that might happen, political and economic, to retard recovery and even to defer it, I have entered upon a slow campaign of selling Jersey and Indiana stock, to at least partially meet the above mentioned commitments.

Mr. Debevoise and Mr. Cutler are in complete agreement with me that under all the circumstances this is the wisest course to pursue, and we are wondering whether a similar course may not commend itself to you, the only difference being that the purpose of your making sales would be to reduce your loan and strengthen your financial position against an unknown future, and not to provide resources with which to meet large commitments, as is true in my case.

Affectionately,
John

Ormond Beach, Florida

---

26 Broadway
New York
February 8, 1933

Dear Father:

In view of the general interest which seems to have been developed in Mr. Flynn's life of you entitled "God's Gold" I have had a new edition of your "Random Reminiscences of Men and Events" printed, and have a thousand copies on hand. I am sending you at Ormond half a dozen copies, thinking you may care to give them to friends from time to time. Do not hesitate to let me know if you want more copies for any number can be supplied. Since all of our children have been so interested in "God's Gold" I am sending each of them a copy of "Random Reminiscences".

David arrived Monday night, enthusiastic over his visit to Ormond. It has done him a great deal of good and he enjoyed every moment of it. Again our thanks for your having so kindly taken him in when the house was not only full but overflowing.

Abby is better although still in bed. She is making very definite progress and we are hoping within a few days will have completely eradicated the infection.

I went to Washington yesterday to a dinner at the White House last night, and was sorry Abby could not go with me. It was a very pleasant affair and I thoroughly enjoyed it.

Affectionately,
John

Ormond Beach, Florida

John T. Flynn, God's Gold: The Story of Rockefeller and His Times *(New York, 1932).*

John D. Rockefeller, Some Random Reminiscences of Men and Events *(New York, 1908; reprinted by Fordham University Press, 1991). The work originally appeared in the Doubleday magazine* World's Work.

26 Broadway
New York
June 28, 1933

Dear Father:

You asked a week or two ago whether we had any suggestions to make in regard to a statement from you on your birthday. I found myself in doubt as to whether a statement this year would be wise and sent you word yesterday that my judgement was rather against it.

Subsequently there occurred to me two or three things of public importance which I felt you might wisely and helpfully say at this time. I therefore wrote down the brief statement which I enclose. This morning I discussed it with Mr. Raymond Fosdick, who was unqualifiedly favorable to something of that kind. I will discuss it with Mr. Lee tomorrow and let you know his reaction. An expression of gratitude from you at the signs of returning prosperity would give confidence to the public; an expression of appreciation of President Roosevelt from you would, it seems to me, be very wise and tactful; while for a man in your position on his ninety-fourth birthday, who might be expected to be living in the past, to sound a note of forward-looking world cooperation, when national selfishness is being exhibited on so many sides, would, I cannot but feel, have a very real influence for good.

These are the reasons why I am submitting this rough draft of a possible statement, that you may be thinking of it even prior to such further corrections and refinements as I may later send you. Of course this is merely a suggestion, and if you decide that it is better to make no statement, I will fully understand and entirely agree.

Affectionately,
John

Lakewood, N.J.

Mr. Rockefeller did not feel it was necessary for him to say anything at this time.

Seal Harbor
Maine
August 25, 1933

Dear Father:

It was a great pleasure to Abby and me to be at Pocantico again with you and we enjoyed each day of our stay. I am sorry that so many problems intruded themselves and made us rather difficult guests. You and Mrs. Evans were, however, most patient and long suffering. Since everything has worked out all right, I hope you will forget the trouble we made you. Abby is being very careful what she does and is making real gain each day. She has had no setback since the one a few days before we left and is, I feel, now really on the road to better health. It will take a long time and much patience, but now that she realizes what the penalty of overdoing is, I am sure she will do everything in her power not to make that mistake again.

I have had frequent and interesting communications over the telephone with Mr. Teagle and Mr. Hicks in Washington, also with Mr. Lee in New York, all bearing generally on my radio speech which is scheduled for tomorrow, Saturday night at ten o'clock Daylight Savings time. It was feared that General Johnson's position on the labor question might somewhat change the situation and make my speech inappropriate. Quite the contrary has, however, been the case. He could not have come out more strongly and finely for perfect freedom on the part of labor to organize as it likes or not at all as it prefers.

We have had much rain since our return and a great deal of fog; but such weather only makes it easier to be lazy and restful.

Again with truest thanks for your hospitality while we were with you, I am,

Affectionately,
John

Pocantico, Hills, N.Y.

Junior's speech was made in support of the National Industrial Recovery Act.

Room 5600
30 Rockefeller Plaza
New York
February 17, 1934

Dear Father:

It hardly seems possible that you are really at Ormond comfortably installed in your beautiful, bright, sunny room there with the warm sunshine and mild air of the south about you. We are all grateful beyond expression that you were able to make the trip so successfully and that you are now in a climate that will help so materially in your return to complete strength and vigor. The experiences of the past four months, I shall never forget. Your marvelous patience, good cheer, courage and constant thoughtfulness for others throughout have made an indelible impression on us all. Such an example of faith and calm as you have given will be an inspiration to us as long as we live. While I have been deeply distressed at your being housed so long and at the necessary alteration of your plan, as I have said to you on several occasions, our frequent visits during these months have been a joy and happiness to me beyond the power of words to express. Never have I more clearly realized that it matters relatively little what one does in comparison with what one is. What you are and always have been has so dominated and outweighed the circumstances in which you found yourself, that even the wonderful things you have done so constantly throughout life have been overshadowed by the greatness, the strength, the simplicity and the modesty of your personality. No son ever had, during the long years of his father's life, such a marvelous heritage as there has come to me every day from you.

As I review the events of the past, I feel convinced of the wisdom of your waiting until you did before going south and equally convinced as to the wisdom of your going when it was clear that the time had come. Your thoughtful telegrams from Baltimore, Jacksonville and Ormond were most welcome and brought added cause for gratitude. I am so happy that the trip was made in comfort and without undue fatigue. After a few days of quiet and complete rest, you will, I know, build up rapidly.

Winthrop's plans for departure are focused on this afternoon. Everything is in readiness and he goes with high hopes and enthusiasm. The interview with Mr. Moffatt and Mr. Teagle was a pleasant one and is sure to be followed by another. The question under discussion will, I feel sure, be adjusted satisfactorily and without difficulty. I had a two hour talk with Mr. Kingsbury of the California Company on Thursday and learned from him many interesting things although none of them of great importance.

As to the Rivera mural which was removed from the walls of Rockefeller Center a week ago tonight, while many of the artists have publicly registered their criticism, you will doubtless see in the paper tomorrow a letter from Mr. Hugh Robertson to one of the artists setting forth conclusions which he has advised their leaders of in person, on the basis of which their whole attitude will, I believe, be changed and their criticism withdrawn. This letter, prepared in my office yesterday, refers to a fact which has never been made public before, namely, that the picture was obscene and, in the judgement of Rockefeller Center, an offense to good taste. The letter goes on to state that it was for this reason primarily that Rockefeller Center decided to destroy it. The artists talked with had never known this fact. They had not for a moment sought to question our right on that ground to suppress the picture. We are now hoping and believing that the disagreeable public criticism which had been leveled at us the past week will be turned to helpful publicity and a sympathetic understanding of our position.

But I must not let myself run on as though I were talking by your bedside, for this is already a letter of wearying length. While we all send you our love and while we want you to know how much we shall miss you each day, we also want you to know how happy we are in the thought of your beautiful and healthful surroundings, which we are sure will build you up rapidly.

Affectionately,
John

The Casements
Ormond Beach, Florida

Diego Rivera, the Mexican artist, was commissioned to paint a monochromatic mural depicting "man's new possibilities from his new understanding of material things." Instead he painted a deeply colored fresco of venereal germs, red flags, rich people playing cards, and a portrait of Lenin. When asked to alter the fresco he refused. The Rivera fresco was destroyed and replaced by large murals by José Maria Sert.

James A. Moffett was President of Standard Oil of Indiana. Walter C. Teagle was President of Standard Oil (New Jersey). Winthrop Rockefeller was on his way to Texas to work in the oil fields.

Room 5600
30 Rockefeller Plaza
New York
February 28, 1934

Dear Father:

Your telegrams have been most gratifying and reassuring and I thank you for them, especially for the last one bearing your congratulations on the success of the gathering at Williamsburg this last Saturday. I am delighted to know that you are up and dressed so many hours each day and that you have also been out to drive. This surely indicates satisfactory progress. What with the veritable blizzard which struck the north beginning with Sunday, we have been most grateful that you are in a warm climate.

Everything went off most satisfactorily at Williamsburg.

Blanchette and John, also David, went down with me. The General Assembly of Virginia, the Governor and other officers of the state, were all most kindly in their reception of us and the Session which they held in the reconstructed Capitol was dignified, impressive and in every way appropriate. There were some two hundred men in the group and as many wives. The wives could not get into the Capitol but heard the exercises over amplifiers in the theater in Williamsburg. After the morning exercises we gave a luncheon to the entire party, which followed a reception, thus giving us an opportunity to meet and shake hands with each one. In the afternoon the guests visited the several important buildings and went back to Richmond on their special train about five. In his address the Governor made reference to what had been done in the restoration of Williamsburg and also to the far flung philanthropies bearing the name of Rockefeller. In these major references you of course were the one to whom credit was due. I was delighted to have the opportunity of accepting his tribute on your behalf. Those introductory words of mine were extemporaneous and not in the printed reports of my address. I shall hope to have secured them from the stenographer shortly and will send you a copy.

Laurance came home for Washington's Birthday. It seems he has not been doing his work as thoroughly and persistently as he should and now he is pressed with the great amount of back work which is mounting up on him. Whether to keep on at Harvard or transfer to some other law school where he will face fewer distractions and have more constant supervision, or what it might be wise to do, he has been seriously considering. Like Winthrop, he lacks power to concentrate on difficult and routine tasks. He has not meant to shirk but has procrastinated. This situation has seemed quite serious to him but I think he is working it out in his mind wisely and satisfactorily and that he is now proposing to dig in and devote himself exclusively to his work for the balance of the year as he has not done heretofore.

Things are going well at Rockefeller Center. Last night the large Municipal Art Exhibition opened in the Center, which has been able to make available gallery space unprecedented any place: there are six thousand feet of running wall space of pictures on exhibition. The artists are all crazy about it. Many who withdrew because of the Rivera murals have come back and only a Corporal's Guard of eight are still out and they picketed the entrance to the Exhibition last night and marched up and down in the cold streets with their banners in a very futile and unconvincing protest.

We have not been to the country since you left. Last Saturday I was in Williamsburg; the Sunday before we stayed in New York. Moreover the roads have been so blocked by the snow and the going so bad that it seemed wiser to stay here. We miss the quiet days and nights there, however, and are planning to go up this Friday if conditions are satisfactory.

Affectionately,
John

The Casements
Ormond Beach, Florida

Pocantico Hills, N.Y.
June 8, 1934

Dear Father:

It was most thoughtful of you to telephone both to the office and to Pocantico after my return from Lakewood on Tuesday. The message which you received through Mr. Madison by mail on Wednesday morning, I sent you by telephone Tuesday but too late to reach you before Mr. Madison had left.

Going and coming in a parlor car on the Pennsylvania Road via Point Pleasant made the journey very easy and restful and also gave me time to do a good deal of work. I came back feeling better than when I went down. I was in town yesterday but am up here at Tarrytown today, where I am dictating this letter.

In answer to the inquiry contained in your letter just received, may I say that the studies of the possibilities of an underground railroad entrance into New York are still going on. I have not seen Mr. Scott since my return to know what the status of the negotiations are, but will be doing so shortly and will advise you. From other people I have gained the impression that the railroads, while recognizing the need and desirability of such construction, are not favoring it because they fear that even if the Government finances it with reconstruction money, in some way sooner or later the burden will be transferred to them and it would be a burden which they do not feel they could carry. This probably is an indication that the undertaking will not be found practicable.

Affectionately,
John

Lakewood, N.J.

Pocantico Hills
November 30, 1934

Dear Father:

Abby and I went to Boston last Thursday to spend a few days with David and also to see Mary and Laurance. We had lunch with Mary and Laurance in their cunning little house in Cambridge and were delighted with it. It has a sitting room, dining room and kitchen on the first floor, a good sized bedroom and bath, a smaller bedroom and den on the second floor. The children have furnished it tastefully, largely with furniture which Abby has loaned them, partly with wedding presents. They have one servant who comes in at noon each day and takes care of the house and cooks their two meals. She is a marvelous cook and a very satisfactory person. The children get their own breakfast. There is a little garage right next to the house where their car is kept. We were delighted to find Laurance and Mary living so comfortably, so simply and so appropriately. They are very happy and all seems to be going well with them.

David has made many friends, both old and young, in Cambridge and Boston. It is interesting and gratifying to see how many older people like him and are glad to be with him. He in turn is charming with them and is most appreciative of their friendship. Because he has been entertained in many homes most delightfully, David wanted to have Abby and me do some entertaining for him in return. We therefore had two dinners and a luncheon while in Boston, to which principally his older friends were invited. We also visited his college rooms and had lunch with him and his roommates in the college dining hall. David lives with a group of six boys. There are three pairs. Each pair has a sitting room with two bedrooms off of it. The three sitting rooms are adjoining and open into each other. Thus it is that these six boys really live as though on one floor in a family house. The boys are all fine fellows, extraordinarily so. One is a Jew, one is a German, one is the son of a Judge in Boston, one is the grandson of Richard Watson Gelder, the New York editor. They are all earnest, serious, thoughtful, wholesome boys full of fun and enjoying good times but with a worth while purpose and ambition in life and seriously interested in intellectual pursuits and high living. David is fortunate in having gotten in with such a group and is holding up his end in a most commendable way. We stayed until Sunday afternoon when I came back to New York, Abby stopping over with Lucy in Providence until Monday.

I am working at the trust funds for the children. My plans have changed somewhat as to the total amount involved for the more I have thought of the subject, the more strongly I have felt the unwisdom, as regards the three younger children, of passing on to a committee, however high-minded and competent, the responsibility for guiding and counseling the boys currently about their financial affairs and the more I have felt that no consideration would justify my transferring that responsibility from my own hands. I am, therefore, setting up trust funds for the three younger boys, as well as the older children, but in amounts that represent nothing more than the capitalization of their present allowances, leaving it to the future to add to these funds from time to time as the circumstances in each case seem to justify, or to make personal, outright gifts if that seems wiser. This change in program affects only the three younger children. The program for the older children and for Abby is being carried out practically as planned. Since you were good enough to be interested in my earlier thoughts on the subject, I have written the above to bring you up to date.

Nelson left a week ago tonight with his Uncle Winthrop Aldrich and a group of the officers of the Chase Bank to make a trip of a month through the West and South in the interest of extending the relations and connections of the Chase Bank. Nelson was taken along as one of the secretaries and trip managers. He was tremendously keen to go and advises us that he is having the most marvelous time imaginable. I am sure that he will get the greatest possible value from this experience and that it will be exceedingly helpful and stimulating to him.

Things seem to be moving nicely in Rockefeller Center. The elevator employees' strike, which has been brewing and more or less active for several months past in the hands of those who were seeking to extend union recognition, has been a source of no little annoyance to the owners of all buildings in the city. An adjustment has recently been reached, however, which is perhaps as satisfactory as could have been expected and which I trust will terminate the trouble of these past months.

Abby and I came to Pocantico on Wednesday night of this week and are staying until Monday. As you know from my telegram, we had five of the children with us at Thanksgiving luncheon yesterday. This morning your beautiful telegram is received and fills us all with gratitude and appreciation. How can I thank you adequately for it?

The temperature is very high, being sixty. Both yesterday and today have been damp, close and foggy. The grass is very green and the place looks beautiful.

Because we have torn down so many of the old houses on the place and have now completed radical repairs on those that remain, we have found ourselves with more mechanics in various trades than we will continue to need. After careful consideration it has seemed wise to let a few go, to offer some others temporary work as laborers and with old Mr. Nelson, who has been on the place so long, to retire him on a modest pension. These changes were carefully considered, wisely planned and have already been carried through with kindliness, consideration and tact. As a result, even the men who have been dropped feel that they have been most justly and generously treated, while dear old Mr. Nelson and his wife find words inadequate to express their deep appreciation of the consideration shown him. A collateral result of this action is that those men who are retained realize that they are not sure of a life tenure of their positions and that current performance only can justify their retention.

Mr. Debevoise has had several colds of late which have pulled him down. I am hoping that after the first of the year he will get away for a little rest and change. There has been no return of his trouble of last year and, generally speaking, he is in better health than he was then. Mr. Turnbull is doing splendidly. Things are moving nicely in the office.

The meetings of the Rockefeller Foundation and the General Education Board occur the 11th, 12th and 13th of December and are to be held in Williamsburg. Abby and I are planning to go down there next week Friday, to be there a couple of days before the Board members arrive.

I think of you consistently, miss greatly our daily visits of last fall which meant so much to me, but rejoice and am profoundly grateful for your splendid condition and in the fact that you are so comfortably established in Ormond.

Affectionately,
John

Ormond Beach, Florida

Junior established trusts for his children and his wife, Abby, in 1934. Eventually all six were approximately equal in value but at the beginning they varied in value. His wife's trust was for $18.3 million, his daughter Abby, John 3rd, and Nelson's trusts were for $12 million each, while Laurance, Winthrop, and David's were for $50,000 each. The last three were increased to about $16 million in 1935.

Laurance S. Rockefeller married Mary French on August 15, 1934. Abby was visiting her sister Lucy Truman Aldrich in Providence.

Ormond Beach
Florida
December 5, 1934

Dear Son:

Your wonderful letter of November 30th is just received. It fills me with unspeakable gratitude.

I gladly and without question accept your change of program in regard to the children. You know best: yours is the responsibility, and I cannot tell you how grateful I am that it is not mine. The chatter of inexperienced people has very little to do with such important questions as are involved.

All goes well with us. I am steadily improving and am grateful beyond measure. My ears are always open for all that pertains to our common interest, and I am deeply appreciative of your constant remembrance of this in your liberal contributions of information.

We are working night and day to give you happy surprises in your visit, which cannot be too soon to suit us,

With tenderest affection,
Father

30 Rockefeller Plaza
New York

Room 5600
30 Rockefeller Plaza
New York
January 4, 1935

Dear Father:

Mr. King sent me a short time ago the enclosed photostat copy of a page from the register of September 1864 of the St Lawrence Hall Hotel of Montreal, containing your signature. He says in his note about the matter, "My surmise is that this signature was written at the time your father and mother were on their wedding trip. The signature was noted by the Dominion Archivist who had the photostat made for me knowing I would be interested and might wish to send it on to you."

This is to me quite a thrilling document. Your handwriting is just as it is today only a little smaller. I presume it was the custom of the times to register one's wife as "lady". When you have finished with this copy of the register, perhaps you will have it returned to me to be kept with other material having to do with your biography.

Mr. King also sends his best wishes to you for the Holiday Season. He has not been so well of late years, having had a good deal of trouble with arthritis. Late this fall he went abroad for a couple of months and had a good rest. He is better now.

Affectionately.
John

Ormond Beach, Florida

Paris, France
May 14, 1935

Dear Father:

This is the last letter that will reach you before we get home for we are sailing on the Bremen on May 22, and we shall probably arrive in New York the following Monday, the 27th. Paris grows more beautiful every day. There were some warm days, although the weather is still cool generally speaking. The blossoms on the horse chestnut trees are marvelous and the flowers and blossoming plants are beautiful. The country is so lovely and so well and carefully cultivated. As we drive outside the city, we traverse miles of country road lined on either side by flowering fruit trees. We are still negotiating with Mathilde about coming here and have had three telephone talks with her. She, poor child, has rheumatism in her hands which are swelled considerably. It is that that delays her coming. Whether she will really arrive or not before our departure is not yet sure.

Abby had a letter from Bessie Drummond the other day. She is in London with Mrs. Dowling and Lady Drummond for the Jubilee and hoped we were coming over there. Lucy arrives in London this Thursday and we had thought to go there to see her, but have decided not to.

Certain matters we had underway in New York when I left are shaping up, so John writes me. Professor Nevins, the historian at Columbia University, has agreed to write your life. President Butler thinks him the ablest historian and writer in America today. I had a long talk with him before leaving and John has had several since. We all feel he will do a good piece of work and are glad at last to have the matter under way.

Another difficult problem we have been working at is the selection of someone to succeed Dr. Flexner as head of the Rockefeller Institute. The matter has been under serious consideration for many months. The decision seems now to be in favor of Dr. Whipple. Dr. Whipple is head of the Medical School in Rochester which Mr. Eastman founded and to which our Boards have given some millions of dollars. He has been most successful in organizing and conducting that institution. For some years he has been a Trustee of the Rockefeller Foundation. Very quiet and unobtrusive in manner and speech, he is nevertheless outstanding in the field of science and highly regarded at home and abroad. Whether Dr. Whipple will accept the invitation or not I have not heard as yet. Perhaps both of these matters should be regarded as confidential for the present.

I have been twice to the new American church in Paris. When you and Mother brought us as children to Paris years ago, I remember we all went to the American Church. It was then in a little street on this side of the river. The new building is across the river, beautifully located with a large Parish house adjacent, and is beautifully modern and well equipped. It cost some $800,000 and was built just before the depression. While it has all been paid for, the cost of operating the new plant with the depreciated dollar has become a very heavy burden and a difficult problem. Arthur Curtiss James was very much interested in the construction of the new building and we joined quite generously with him in contributing to it.

To our surprise and great satisfaction we observed when in Rome and Naples that no motor horns are blown in the street; the quiet thus resulting is marvelous. An effort to enforce the same ruling is being made in Paris at night and with much success. Even in the day-time, horns are used much less than formerly. I have recently been writing to the secretary of Mayor LaGuardia, whom I know, bringing this matter to his attention and expressing the hope that something of the kind may be done in New York. The experience of these European cities proves that the noise of motor horns is not necessary for safety.

As you probably know Mr. Raymond Fosdick has returned from China and has succeeded in arranging for the closing up of matters there with Mr. Roger Greene as planned. He found the situation very delicate but handled it, I am sure, with great skill and tact. Abby and I dined the other night with Parmalee's sister, Mary Porter and her daughter. You will recall that she married the son of Mr. H. H. Porter of Chicago, but I am not writing more now for I shall hope before many weeks to see you and talk with you about various things that have happened since we left home. Whether you will be at Lakewood when this letter arrives or still at Ormond, I am not sure, but I am sending the letter to Ormond.

Affectionately,
John

Lakewood, N.J.

Allan Nevins wrote two biographies of John D. Rockefeller: John D. Rockefeller: The Heroic Age of American Enterprise *(New York, 1940) and* John D. Rockefeller, Industrialist and Philanthropist *(New York, 1953).*

Mathilde was the daughter of Edith Rockefeller McCormick.

Junior contributed $204,000 toward the construction of the American Church in Paris.

Room 5600
30 Rockefeller Plaza
New York
July 11, 1935

Dear Father:

It has been our privilege to be with you on a great many birthdays. Never have we enjoyed the birthday with you more than this 96th birthday. Our stay in Lakewood was one of the most delightful and restful visits that we have ever made you. Both Abby and I enjoyed every minute of it and came away greatly refreshed and built up as a result.

I cannot tell you how happy it made us to find you so well, so much yourself and, as always, so wonderful a father to us. Our hearts are filled with gratitude for you and for all that you are to us and to the world. These are precious years for us all and we are prizing them and enjoying them and getting the most out of them as they go by.

Bab and Dave, John and Blanchette dined with us last night. Bab and Dave are going to Bermuda this weekend for a few days. They are thinking of buying a little place and building a bungalow there where they can go for rest and quiet and take the children vacation times. John and Blanchette are leaving for Maine tomorrow and will be with us there for several weeks. We had yesterday splendid letters from Nelson and Laurance telling of their quiet, restful ocean voyage and safe arrival.

These last days in the office have been very busy but I am leaving with things in good shape. We shall be tonight at the Ritz-Carlton in Boston and shall motor tomorrow and Saturday on to Maine, arriving in Seal Harbor Saturday night.

Yesterday Professor Nevins, who is working on your biography, had lunch with me and we had a very interesting and satisfactory talk. The Professor finds himself increasingly interested in this new undertaking which he says is one of the most fascinating projects on which he has ever worked. Perhaps when

I am here in August and come down to spend a night or two with you, you may feel like having me bring the Professor with me just that he may shake your hand and look into your face.

Your birthday photographs are meeting with great success. Mr. Todd, one of the managers of Rockefeller Center, was in my office the other morning and I showed him the photograph. He was perfectly delighted with it and said nothing would give him greater pleasure than to have one. I gladly gave him the photograph and told him I knew you would be pleased to have him have it. Since then Mr. Cutler and Mr. Debevoise have made similar requests which I have granted on your behalf. It is a joy to have these lovely pictures. Thank you for the two which I have ventured to keep myself.

Affectionately,
John

Lakewood, N.J.

Lakewood, N.J.
July 12, 1935

Dear Son:

Your ever welcome letter of the 11th just at hand and is a great comfort and delight to us all. We will be pleased to see the historian with you as suggested, and we welcome the flight of time til then. We could not have enjoyed a visit more than the last. With tenderest affection for you and dear Abby with all the children,

Father

Seal Harbor, Maine

Room 5600
30 Rockefeller Plaza
New York
September 11, 1935

Dear Father:

My visit to you over the weekend, so prolonged and leisurely, was a great delight and I go back to Maine with happiest memories of you and our various talks together. Professor Nevins' coming was a great success from his point of view and mine. To have seen you as he did in so natural a way will be a real inspiration to him as he enters upon the work of writing your biography.

This has been a very busy ten days but very satisfactory on the whole. Many things have been consummated and I go back to Maine with a sense of satisfaction and in a frame of mind that will permit my making these remaining weeks there most restful and carefree. Nelson and Mary are going with us. David will come up and also Laurance and his wife. Our visit with Winthrop has been in every way happy and satisfactory. He goes to St. Louis to be an usher at a wedding tomorrow and then back to Texas.

It was so beautiful at Pocantico this morning with the grass a vivid green, the trees more healthy than they have been in years, the sky so bright that I hated to come away. We leave tonight and will be in Seal Harbor tomorrow morning.

Yesterday I had a couple of hours with Dr. Gasser who succeeds Dr. Flexner as head of the Rockefeller Institute. I was immensely pleased with him from every point of view and feel sure he is going to fill the position with great distinction and satisfaction to us all.

I shall be in New York the first week of October to keep several appointments and shall look forward to seeing you at that time.

With truest thanks for the happiness of the weekend and much love, I am,

Affectionately,
John

Lakewood, N.J.

Herbert S. Gasser, winner of the Nobel Prize in 1944, was director of the Rockefeller Institute from 1935 to 1953.

Room 5600
30 Rockefeller Plaza
New York, N.Y.
October 28, 1935

Dear Father:

I came back from Williamsburg last night on the night train to appear before the Special Committee of the Rockefeller Foundation appointed to consider Jerome Greene's charges and to deal with the resignation of Dr. Mason. The Committee meets this morning, is to see Mr. Greene this afternoon and I am to appear before it this evening at dinner. While I hate to interrupt my stay in Williamsburg, these other matters are most important and I feel sure that they will now be dealt with in a way that will clear the air and prevent any further necessity of their consideration.

Abby and I with Laurance and Mary arrived in Williamsburg last Friday morning. Bab and Dave and Nelson arrived Saturday morning and Winthrop Aldrich and his wife Saturday afternoon. We had wonderfully beautiful days and a most delightful family gathering. Bab, Laurance and Mary came back with me. Nelson leaves this morning and Harriet and Winthrop this afternoon. I am going back on the night train tonight to join Abby there tomorrow morning to remain for the balance of the week. We are increasingly gratified with the results of our labors in Williamsburg and are venturing to believe more and more that what has been done there is fully justified and will be a real contribution to the development of a growing appreciation of the founders of this country. As we visited the prison at Williamsburg, recently restored, and saw the rooms set aside for debtors, I could not but think how the times have changed. In the early days of this country a debt was regarded not only as a matter of honor, but as strictly enforceable under the law and those who did not pay their debts were imprisoned. Today, as a result of what we like to think of as the advancement of civilization, an example is set us as a nation by the chief executive officer minimizing the sacredness of a promise and seeking to justify the repudiation of one's financial obligations. What a commentary on life!

Your letter of October 21st was most welcome as well as your telegram of the 24th. I hope it is a little cooler in Ormond and that you are being able to be outdoors a great deal. The conductor on the train coming up from Richmond last night told me that he had taken you down to Ormond and spoke with great enthusiasm of you.

Affectionately,
John

Ormond, Florida

Room 5600
30 Rockefeller Plaza
New York, N.Y.
November 7, 1935

Dear Father:

Thank you for your telegrams of the 31st and the 6th, both of which were greatly appreciated. We had a delightful ten days but dull, muggy and rainy weather toward the end. However, there are so many things in Williamsburg that interest us that the weather never makes any particular difference. On Saturday last the College had its annual Home Day for the alumni. A parade was gotten up with many floats representing different historical scenes, in which the college students both boys and girls took part. In the parade was the old coach of the revolutionary period, which we have bought and have done over just as it was in those days, driven by a colored coachman with a footman standing on behind, both in gorgeous blue livery of the day with knee breeches, buckled shoes and cocked hats. In the coach, the windows of which were open, sat four really lovely hostesses of our exhibition houses, all dressed in the costumes of the period. I wish you could have seen what a charming picture the whole combination made.

My meeting a week ago Monday with the special committee of the Foundation appointed to consider Mr. Greene's charges of the control of the Foundation by our office was held at my house at dinner that night. Mr. John W. Davis, the lawyer, is the Chairman of the committee; President Hopkins of Dartmouth and Dr. Whipple of the Medical School of Rochester are the other members. Mr. Debevoise was also present. That day Mr. Greene had presented to the committee a memorandum setting forth his views and had spent a number of hours discussing it with the committee. Mr. Davis told us that as the committee went over point by point Mr. Greene's memorandum and developed his thought with him, it was interesting to see how he seemed to feel less and less insistent on his position and more and more in agreement with the committee. The opportunity to have formally presented his views to an unbiased group has of itself afforded an outlet to Mr. Greene which will go far toward satisfying him. The committee did not find itself sympathetic with the suggestions which he made and will tactfully but clearly so indicate in its final report. Instead of agreeing with Mr. Greene as to the harmfulness of such contact as there is between our office and the Foundation the committee felt that the relationship which exists is not only proper but highly desirable for the Foundation. I think, therefore, that while much time and effort are being spent in dealing with Mr. Greene's proposals, it will all prove worthwhile in the end.

The question of Dr. Mason's successor as President of the Foundation is being seriously considered as well as Mr. Arnett's retirement as President of the General Education Board. The nominating committees of the two Boards met with me at luncheon yesterday. Mr. Greene is Chairman of the General Education

Board nominating committee. We had a most friendly and amiable discussion. The committees feel that the best interests of the two Boards will be served by having the same man as President of each and they also feel that Mr. Raymond Fosdick is the man best fitted to fill this dual position. While it is too early to predict, I think there is every prospect that the committees will recommend his election in the December meetings of the two Boards. This is in line with a feeling which has been growing on me for some years past. I think it will be an ideal arrangement if Mr. Fosdick is willing to accept the dual appointment, as I am inclined to believe he will be. You will see, therefore, that we are making progress with these difficult questions and that it looks as though they would be worked out without bitterness and to the general satisfaction of all—for which I am most grateful.

Last night Abby and I dined with Mr. Blumenthal to meet the French Ambassador and his wife. About thirty people were present and we had a delightful evening.

Dr. Walker of Cleveland spent a number of hours with me the week after my return from Lakewood and we discussed the Cleveland church problem from every point of view. Instead of asking Mr. Packard of our office to study the problem for the church, it developed as a result of my talk with Dr. Walker that a certain Dr. Douglass, whose writing on city church problems Dr. Walker had found most helpful, should be asked to make the study. This I agreed to pay for and it is to be made at an early date. Dr. Walker was greatly pleased to have this expert judgement brought to bear on the problem and I have had a letter from the Board of Trustees of the church expressing their appreciation. I had hoped that Dr. Walker would feel that he could defer decision regarding his call to California until after this report had been made and some conclusions as to the further policy of the church reached. To my regret, however, I have recently heard from him—as you undoubted have—that he has resigned, the resignation to take effect the end of this year. That the Cleveland church should get on some basis of operation within the limit of its own ability to support, seems to me vital to its future life and usefulness. That the study being made by this Dr. Douglass will lead to the discovery of that basis and to its adoption by the church, is my earnest hope. You may rest assured that I am giving the matter full and careful consideration and will follow it closely.

Affectionately,
John

Ormond Beach, Florida

Room 5600
30 Rockefeller Plaza
New York, N.Y.
November 29, 1935

Dear Father:

You have seen probably in the papers recently reference to my having discontinued giving to the Northern Baptist Convention to which you and I have contributed for so many years. This decision I have been coming to as a result of five years of careful thought and study. It was because of my doubt as to the wise use of the moneys thus given for home and foreign missions that I took steps to bring about the study of the foreign missions which was completed a year or two ago. I found that Mr. Ballard, Dr. Fosdick and others shared my doubts about the efficiency and present value of many of these missionary efforts. They were as glad as I to have this study made so that they might know the facts. As you know, the report made by the Commission confirmed our fears but pointed out cooperative ways in which, with a more modest appropriation, an infinite amount of good could be done in the mission fields.

I hoped that the Baptist missionary societies would appreciate the information which this report put at their disposal and would be disposed to follow its recommendations. This they have not been willing to do although several other denominations have. After patiently working with them in an effort to win their support of the new program and after giving them full notice of my intentions, I reached the conclusion that there was nothing left for me to do but to discontinue giving through the Northern Baptist Convention and to make gifts directly to those missionary efforts—whether Baptist, of other denominations, interdenominational or non-denominational—that have proved themselves to us as vital, effective, Christian agencies.

My letter, recently published, was written last March. Somehow the Press recently got hold of the fact that such a letter existed and when it developed that a garbled article was to be published, it seemed best for us to give out the letter since the Northern Baptist Convention people declined to do so. This we finally did, they consenting. Although you may have seen the letter in the newspapers I am sending you a printed copy of it should you care to reread it sometime at your convenience. I am sure you will know that this step was not taken by me without the fullest conference with wise advisors and then only after years of patient waiting and kindly effort to win the Baptist missionary societies to a more modern and efficient missionary program. I hope you will not disapprove.

Affectionately,
John

Ormond Beach, Florida

The report Re-Thinking Missions *was published in the fall of 1932 by the Layman's Foreign Missions Inquiry, an ecumenical group financed in part by Junior, which spent a year studying American missions in China, Japan, and India.*

Ormond Beach, Florida
December 5, 1935

Dear Son:

Answering yours of November 29th received with letter enclosed as stated, I had not followed the question, and regret all the trouble it has made for you. My confidence is not at all shaken that you would not have acted with thorough deliberation and most commendable consideration, and I hope that everything will come out all right.

With tenderest affection,
Father

30 Rockefeller Plaza
New York

Room 5600
30 Rockefeller Plaza
New York
December 5, 1935

Dear Father:

You will be interested to know that the situation in Forest Hill real estate development is greatly improved over last year. All of the apartments in the apartment house are rented but one and all of the houses occupied. A few of them have been sold; most of them are rented. Several stores only are vacant. In the case of the houses, we have increased rents and are expecting to increase them still further next year as leases expire.

The result of this improvement in conditions is that whereas in 1933 my real estate committee asked me to approve a net budget of $235,000 to carry the property and this year a net budget of $127,000, it is asking next year for a budget of $81,000. The gross budget is $215,000. the probable income $134,000. The committee is most optimistic about the future and believes that 1936 is going to show a marked improvement in the situation. It is a pleasure to be able to pass on to you this good news.

Affectionately
John

Ormond Beach, Florida

The Forest Hill estate was divided into two parts. One part was given as a park to the local community. Junior developed the other part with homes, an apartment building, and offices and stores. It was never an economic success.

Room 5600
30 Rockefeller Plaza
New York
December 7, 1935

Dear Father:

You may have seen in the papers recently reference to an apartment building operation which we are about to enter upon in the development of the property which we own across the street from our present house in 54th Street and extending through to 55th Street. The enclosed newspaper clipping gives some interesting illustrations.

This is the first step in a program which we have been studying for a long time, having in mind how best ultimately to develop and put on a paying basis the large amount of real estate which we have accumulated adjacent to and in the vicinity of No. 4 and No. 10. If these apartment houses are successful, it would be in our minds to build a number of others on adjoining lands which we own. The idea has been well received by the public and the publicity which the announcement has brought ought to be helpful.

As you will realize, there has been practically no building of apartment houses since the depression began. We are informed that there is, therefore, already a very real and growing demand for apartments. The two houses which we are building will face, one on 54th Street, the other on 55th Street, and will have a common garden in the rear of both. They will be ten or twelve stories high, will have every modern convenience and yet will be simply and not expensively constructed. They are not intended for families but rather for the large number of people who either live alone or with a husband or wife or one friend and do not want to be tied down to housekeeping.

I shall be glad to tell you more about this project when I see you.

Affectionately,
John

Ormond Beach, Florida

Room 5600
30 Rockefeller Plaza
New York
December 9, 1935

Dear Father:

We are trying to make space enough in the basement under the garage and stable at Pocantico so that another year it will be possible to discontinue the orange house and to store in this basement, which is heated of necessity as part of the building, such trees as we may still have on hand that have been heretofore stored in the orangerie. In working toward that end, I find in the basement of the garage three cars of yours—two of them touring cars, one a limousine—which have not been used for some years and which I fancy are permanently out of service.

Would it be entirely agreeable to you to have me dispose of these cars?

Affectionately,
John

Ormond Beach, Florida

The cars were disposed of with Mr. Rockefeller Senior's permission.

Room 5600
30 Rockefeller Plaza
December 13, 1935
New York, N.Y

Dear Father:

You will be glad to know that the opening of the Frick Collection took place on Wednesday and was a great success from every point of view. Eighteen hundred people were asked. About half the number came. Everyone seemed immensely pleased and greatly admired the beauty of the works of art presented in the setting of the home of the original owner. On this coming Monday the public will be admitted and from then on. It is a satisfaction to have so unqualifiedly successful an outcome of the work to which with others I have been giving myself in considerable degree for the last three or four years. I am sure Mr. Frick would be greatly pleased with the result and the appreciation of the public.

We have just had the meetings of the Foundation and the General Education Board. Dr. Mason's resignation as President of the Foundation was accepted and Mr. Fosdick was elected President of both Boards, to take office the first of July next. The report of the Special Committee, appointed to consider the various matters raised by Mr. Greene, was wholly in approval of the present management and organization and contained only minor suggestions of change. Action on the report was deferred until the next meeting, copies of it to be sent to the Trustees in the meantime. Mr. Greene seemed entirely happy and satisfied. Thus, the meetings went off very successfully and satisfactorily. To have Mr. Fosdick take up the work of these two Boards will mean much to the Boards and to me as your representative. I feel no one could be chosen who would be more in sympathy with the principles of the Boards than Mr. Fosdick, nor anyone easier to work with, more cooperative, wiser and generally liked. It is a very happy outcome. This, of course, will terminate Mr. Fosdick's personal relation to our office but in a sense it means merely his transfer to full time in the Foundations to which he has long been giving no small part of his time.

As a matter of record, I went to the Rockefeller Institute last week to have the usual examinations. I learned this morning that my heart photographs indicate an absolutely normal heart. For some time I have been anaemic and have taken liver—in fact for some years. Last spring I stopped the liver. The blood test just taken shows the blood count to be absolutely normal and perfectly free from anaemia, in spite of the fact that I have taken no liver for the past six months. This can only be accounted for on the ground that my general condition is better that it has been for some time. Perhaps this all indicates that I should do more work rather than less. In any event it is gratifying. Abby is much better and practically all over her cold but still somewhat weak and confined to the house.

I am looking forward eagerly to being with you the end of next week.

Affectionately,
John

Ormond Beach, Florida

Ormond Beach
Florida
December 16, 1935

Dear Son:

I cannot express my joy and satisfaction on the receipt of your letter of the 13th. Let us rejoice in the most devout thanksgiving. We are filled with delight in anticipating your visit. All goes well with us and we unite in every best wish for you all. With tenderest affection,

Father

26 Broadway
New York

Ormond Beach
Florida
January 2, 1936

Dear Son:

I greatly enjoyed and profited by your beautiful letter of December 30th just received. Everybody at Casements is always happy to have you come and sorry to have you go, and we all have that delightful feeling in reference to David. He is so helpful to everyone and we are sorry that he is going back so soon. All goes well with us and we are taking great care about diet and rest and all. How richly we are paid for the little thoughtful observances. We are so grateful to be in such close touch on the wire and in every way.

With tenderest affection,
Father

30 Rockefeller Plaza
New York

The Ritz-Carlton
Boston, Mass.
January 22, 1936

Dear Father:

When I wrote you the other day I neglected to thank you for your beautiful letter of January 2nd in which you spoke so sweetly of David's visit, and how you had all enjoyed it. David loves being with you and loves talking with you, and if he is able to do his part in bringing interest and being of service, he is only the happier.

You will remember I talked with you about the young Princeton tutor, a friend of John Archbold, who is writing the life of John's grandfather, Mr. Archbold. I told you that I had some correspondence with Anne Archbold about the matter. She was anxious that the life should be a wholly accurate one, and eager for any help that we could give her to that end. The result was that I got Mr. Inglis to read Mr. Moore's manuscript.

When I was in Ormond I read you Mr. Inglis' memorandum on the manuscript, pointing out the fact that generally speaking Mr. Moore seemed to take the Tarbell attitude and calling attention to several stories about you and Mr. Archbold that were neither true or worthy of inclusion.

Just before leaving New York, as I wrote you, Mr. Inglis lunched with Mr. Nevins, your biographer, and his assistant, at my invitation and we all had a most satisfactory talk. Since then Mr. Inglis has had a number of conferences with Mr. Moore, has discussed fully with him his manuscript on Mr. Archbold, and has just written me a letter, of which I enclose a copy. This I am sure you will read with much interest and satisfaction. All of this will help with your biography, for as you know, as the head Professor of history at Columbia University he will have to pass on Mr. Moore's life of Mr. Archbold. I feel delighted about the whole thing, and I am sure you will be also.

Affectionately,
John

Ormond Beach, Florida

Inglis wrote that he and Mr. Moore had studied Senior's career from the earliest days as recorded in the material Inglis had accumulated between 1917 and 1936. Inglis quoted Moore as saying, "I can see that I was misled from the beginning; that Mr Rockefeller was intent on stabilizing a wild industry, not only for his own protection but for the welfare of all who would join the organization for mutual benefit. I shall have to re-write all that part of my book."

Inglis went on to say that Moore agreed to cut out "the button-hook incident, the poker story and similar errors." "I believe he is sincere, and I like him," Inglis concluded.

The biography of John D. Archbold was published by the Columbia University Press in 1948. Austin Leith Moore, John D. Archbold and the Early Development of the Standard Oil Company.

The Ritz-Carlton
Boston, Mass.
January 27, 1936

Dear Father:

Your letter of the twenty-fifth is just received. It is most thoughtful of you to make mention of the invitation to the Musicale which we are giving next month for Blanchette and Mary. The invitation was sent because we wanted you to know that we would like to have had you with us on that occasion, and because we knew you would be interested in our plan to give these two daughters-in-law the same sort of an introduction to our friends that we gave Nelson's wife four or five years ago. We are asking about five hundred people, although we are not expecting that more than two hundred will come.

I am enclosing a copy of a letter from Dr. Hartwell, which I am sure you will enjoy. Dr. Hartwell is a leading New York surgeon who has done much professional work in connection with the Rockefeller Institute, and has always been most helpful to the Institute.

I brought down with me several boxes of old letters which I have been reading over. Among them I have found a treasure trove, namely a sealed envelope which Aunt Lute left for me, and which contains eleven letters in your own handwriting, written to mother between the years '68 and '72. They tell many things about your business interviews, your plans, your purposes, and the individuals whom you were seeing. They will be invaluable in connection with your biography, and because they show, as has never been shown, what your purpose was in bringing those oil companies together, and how all you ever sought was that which was right and fair. The letters are also sweet and lovely in the affection for mother and the children which they evince. I am having them copied so that the originals can be carefully preserved, and will bring copies with me to Ormond to read you. I know you will find them immensely interesting.

I have also run across three letters to me from grandmother Rockefeller, one written in her own hand. These in their way are equally interesting and valuable.

We are getting on nicely here, but it seems wise to remain one week longer instead of returning to New York this Saturday as planned.

Affectionately
John

Ormond Beach, Florida

Ormond Beach
Florida
January 27, 1936

Dear Son:

Thanks for you beautiful and most acceptable letter of the 27th with enclosures so full of interest and comfort. All goes well with us. Pleased you are delaying your stay for the health and hope it will prove the best thing in every way.

With tenderest affection for each and every one of you,

Father

The Ritz-Carlton
Boston, Mass

Room 5600
30 Rockefeller Plaza
New York
February 20, 1936

Dear Father:

The musicale for Blanchette and Mary, Laurance's wife, was a great success. Two hundred and twenty-five people came. Lily Pons, one of the most popular opera singers of the present day, with a gorgeous voice and a charming personality, sang exquisitely and a young French cellist played with equal skill and charm. Abby and the two girls were simply adorable in their new gowns gotten for the occasion and were worth coming to see even if there had been no musical program. John and Laurance helped make the people feel at home and showed them to their seats. They could not have been more gracious and cooperative. Many people have spoken and written of their enjoyment of the evening, of the extraordinarily delightful group of people gathered there, of the charm of the three ladies and of the hospitality shown them by all the family, as well as of the unusually beautiful musical program.

Bab and Dave and the little girls are enthusiastic about their stay with you although some of them brought back colds caught the last cold day. It was lovely of you and Mrs. Evans to take them all in. I am delighted that Mr. Raymond Fosdick has come back to you for a few days. From the outset I felt sure that no place would he get more complete rest and refreshment of the body and spirit than in your house and from what he has written to me that has proved to be the case.

The weather is still cold and wintry here. Things are going well with just enough of current problems to make life interesting. The Frick Collection is operating most successfully but the friction resulting from the family's desire to dominate the situation makes constant difficulty and has so exhausted our splendid director that he has handed in his resignation. He is away now for a three month's vacation and before his return I am hoping that the Trustees may have taken certain definite steps that will prevent a continuation of the difficulties which have so worn him out and that he may be persuaded to withdraw his resignation.

Thank you for your telegram of the 10th in answer to my letter. That you keep so well in spite of the cold weather makes us all most grateful. By the way Alta came to our musicale and brought with her Della Prentiss although Parmalee was unable to come.

The complete report on the Euclid Avenue Baptist Church situation has been received and I have read it with much interest. What course the Trustees will decide to pursue will shortly be determined. When I see you I shall probably by able to advise you what action they have taken. The temporary minister who is supplying the pulpit and who, as you know, is the same person who supplied the pulpit in California to which Dr. Walker went, is proving an excellent man and is holding the church together admirably. Unfortunately he is sixty-five years of age and could not be thought of as the permanent pastor.

Affectionately,
John

Ormond Beach, Florida

Ormond Beach
Florida
February 24, 1936

Dear Son:

Your unspeakably good letter of the 20th just at hand and deeply appreciated. Many thanks. All is going well with us and we are counting the days until you and Abby come. All of you take good care of yourselves.

With tenderest affection,
Father

Room 5600
30 Rockefeller Plaza
New York

John D. Rockefeller died on May 23, 1937 at his home in Florida. Five weeks earlier he had written Junior about plans for a wedding present for the son of his daughter Alta Rockefeller Prentice. With Junior's approval he decided to make the gift to a trust set up for the grandson. He addressed this letter, dated April 13, 1937, as always: "Dear Son." He concluded it saying, "All goes well with us and we unite in every best wish for you and Abby and all the rest. With tenderest affection, Father."

EPILOGUE: THE STEWARDSHIP IN ACTION

From 1907 to 1937 Edith Rockefeller McCormick, Senior's second daughter, compiled scrapbooks of press articles on her father's life. The collection, some 200 oversized volumes of about 200 pages each, is at the Rockefeller Archive Center. Favorable and unfavorable articles from newspapers and periodicals, and editorial cartoons, jostle each other on the many pages. The last three volumes, compiled after Rockefeller's death, are different. Almost without exception, publications from around the world sing the praises of Rockefeller the philanthropist, the builder of a great company, the founder of the Rockefeller Foundation, the General Education Board, the Rockefeller Institute for Medical Research, and the University of Chicago. The contents of these three volumes describe the public legacy that Rockefeller, Senior, bequeathed to his son—a public legacy as significant as the private one transmitted through the fifty years of correspondence between father and son.

Five intensely personal themes run through these letters. There is the intimate respect and love shared among the members of the family. There are the instructions and cautions of a father to his growing son. The son's willingness to accept the father's precepts and examples reflects the reverse side of this theme. There is the son's conscious assumption of the responsibilities resulting from a family fortune that approached $990 million in 1912, responsibilities that were increasingly transferred to the son. Finally, there is the overriding faith in a benevolent God.

In 1895 Rockefeller Senior wrote, "We rejoice that you know from experience that good for you is inseparately connected with the good you bring to others. But this is not a lecture, only a kind word from an affectionate father to a much loved and only son on the occasion of his 21st birthday." The letter enclosed a birthday gift of $21.

By 1922 Senior had given Junior over $465 million. The large gifts were made between 1916 and 1922. Midstream during the transfer of the fortune, Senior wrote, "What a Providence that your life should have been spared to take up the responsibilities as I lay them down. . . . I am indeed blessed beyond measure in having a son whom I can trust to do this most particular and most important work. Go carefully. Be conservative. Be sure you are right—and then do not be afraid to give out, as your heart prompts you, and as the Lord inspires you."

The stream of instruction and inspiration from father to son was received with humility. "May God grant me strength to follow in your footsteps, with the same sweetness of spirit, the same generosity of heart and the same wisdom which has been so characteristic of your life." The personal bond between father and son is expressed best in their thoughts on fulfilling their responsibilities flowing from the fortune.

But there are other aspects of the relationship reflected in the correspondence. The conception, creation, and nurturing of the Rockefeller Institute for Medical Research, the General Education Board, and the Rockefeller Foundation are outlined in these letters. Junior was the efficient go-between who turned the dreams of F. T. Gates, William Rainey Harper, William W. Welch, and other reformers into reality by guiding Senior's gift-giving.

Junior, however, was not always successful in guiding his father's thoughts. In 1921 officers of the Standard Oil Company (New Jersey) wanted to increase the annual dividends. Although his protest was unsuccessful, Senior urged that Junior try to thwart the plan. "It will be easy enough to increase dividends later, when we see that all is safe, but I am convinced that the conservative policy we pursued in the old days in the financing of the oil companies is the right one and I am very desirous that we should not depart from it. . . . The prime factor is, as I state, to keep the concern strong, prosperous, vigorous, aggressive, on its own feet and on its own merits. Then it can borrow money. Then it can sell stock. But the tail must not wag the dog, and the business must be conducted primarily for the good of the concern itself, and only then will the best interest of every stockholder be conserved."

Alongside the business and philanthropic concerns, the letters portray the ever-changing life and activities of a growing family. Between 1887 and 1897 there are sleigh rides and ice skating. Screen doors are painted and horses are bridled. Rockefeller Senior testifies before Congress on the Standard Oil Trust, and the first gift is made to the new University of Chicago. In 1893 Junior enters Brown University, where he finds new social dimensions, a future wife, and an education.

The second decade, 1897–1907, brings Junior into his father's personal office. He becomes one of three advisors to Senior, the others being F. T. Gates and Starr J. Murphy. He speculates on the stock market and loses "hundreds of thousands of dollars," which his father replaces. He assists in the negotiations of the terms for the creation of the large Rockefeller philanthropies.

Junior marries Abby Aldrich and their first two children are born, Abby and John D. 3rd. His salary reaches $10,000 a year, an amount he is sure he is not worthy to receive. He suggests his father provide financial support for Junior's sister, Alta, and her new husband, E. Parmelee Prentice. Senior agrees to provide funds for the purchase of blankets, brushes, brooms, and the other "thousand and one little things required for the operation of a house." He also provides the house.

Between 1907 and 1916 Junior and the office staff diversify the fortune from an emphasis on oil companies, railroads, and real estate into holdings in banks, insurance companies, and additional railroads. Senior gives some shares in the Standard Oil Company (New Jersey) to his three living children but cautions them not to sell the stock without informing him. He also gives Junior his entire holding in the American Linseed Company and some real estate in New York City. This decade is also a period when Junior's family expands: four sons are born: Nelson Aldrich in 1908, Laurance S. in 1910, Winthrop in 1912, and David in 1915. Junior builds a new home for his growing family at 10 West 54th Street, adjacent to his father's town house at 4 West 54th. He buys a large home in Seal Harbor, Maine, and expands his home on the family estate in Pocantico Hills, New York.

Between 1917 and 1922 Senior gives Junior over $425 million in cash, bonds, and securities. Senior's letters of transmittal and Junior's letters of gratitude are brilliant examples of simplicity. No extra words are needed when the gift is for $1 million in cash or $20 million in bonds.

The twenty years, 1917–1937, bring subtle changes in the correspondence. The care of homes in Florida, New Jersey, New York, and Maine become matters of growing concern. Senior's portrait is painted twice by John Singer Sargent, Paul Manship creates a marble bust, and William O. Inglis preserves Senior's recollections in type. Senior continues his interest in the affairs of the oil industry and the world around him but he prefers to be an observer rather a participant.

Junior's letters are filled with his growing universe of action. He buys land for Ft. Tryon park in northern Manhattan and finances the building of Rockefeller Center and the tower of Riverside Church. He begins the restoration of Colonial Williamsburg and of cultural monuments in France and China, and builds a museum in Jerusalem. Believing that worthwhile places enrich the soul of man, he makes America's national parks one of his main beneficiaries. His largesse spreads across the nation; from Acadia in Maine to the Grand Tetons in Wyoming, from the redwoods of California to the pines of the Great Smoky Mountains and Shenandoah, he contributes millions of dollars and hours of personal concern and thought.

The 1920s also see Junior enter the public forum with his vision of necessary changes in the religious and business climate of America. He challenges the "fundamentalists" of the Northern Baptist Convention, not only with words but with action by withdrawing his past substantial financial support and throwing that support to the religious liberals represented by Harry Emerson Fosdick and the Riverside Church.

Speaking clearly and with confidence, Junior challenges the existing ethics of the business community. He mounts a widely publicized proxy fight to drive Col. Robert W. Stewart from the chairmanship of the Standard Oil Company of Indiana when Stewart proves less than honest in his testimony before a Congressional committee. Echoes of this challenge can be seen in the access oil industry leaders find to Senior though Junior.

Senior withdraws gradually into a golfing routine which moves with the seasons from Florida to New Jersey to New York and back. Family matters grow in importance in the letters. Junior's family, now consisting of one daughter and five sons, emerges from young adulthood and the six enter the economic, social, and political establishment. Each major turning point in their lives is shared with Senior. As concern about Senior's health grows, family visits to Florida and New Jersey become more frequent. Senior looks forward to such visits. The exchange of gifts continues at Christmas and birthdays. They range from a Crane-Simplex and the cash value of a Rolls Royce to golf balls, tie pins, handkerchiefs, and cravats. The last letter in this selection refers to the proper size of a wedding gift to a grandchild.

Both Rockefellers strove to live up to the ideal of stewardship presented in these letters. Senior gave over $480 million to the Rockefeller philanthropic organizations and another $58 million to schools and colleges and to religious and welfare organizations. He gave about $500 million to members of his family, most of it to Junior. While the bulk of Senior's giving was directed to the Rockefeller philanthropies, Junior diversified his giving dramatically. Of his $537 million in philanthropic giving, he gave $192 million to Rockefeller philanthropic organizations, such as the Rockefeller Brothers Fund, the International Education Board, the Bureau of Social Hygiene, and the Sealantic Fund, but he gave over $345 million to other organizations and causes. Of this total, $121 million went toward cultural and conservation activities such as the national parks, Colonial Williamsburg, the Metropolitan Museum of Art, and Lincoln Center for the Performing Arts. Brown, Harvard, and New York universities, Barnard and Spelman colleges, the Massachusetts Institute of Technology, the New York Public Library, the United Negro College Fund, and the International Houses in New York and Paris were the largest recipients of the $106 million given toward education. The $72 million given to religious organizations was spread among the YM and YWCAs, the Riverside Church in New York, the National Council of Churchs, and the Union Theological Seminary, as well many smaller congregations and organizations. The second largest recipient of Rockefeller Junior's giving was the Rockefeller Brothers Fund. Organized by his five sons in 1940, the Fund was created to rationalize the giving of the diverse group. Junior gave the Fund $58 million in 1952 and one half of his estate, over $70 million, went to the Fund after his death in 1960.

He gave $261 million to members of his family, primarily through trusts that endure across several generations.

John D. Rockefeller and his son John D. Rockefeller, Jr., shared in the adventure once described by Senior as an effort toward making a better world. This is the legacy of their understanding of their stewardship.

SOURCES

The letters in this collection were selected from Record Group 1 (Letterbooks, 1877–1918) and Record Group 2 (John D. Rockefeller, Jr. Personal Papers, Boxes) of the Rockefeller Family Archives. The family archives are now at the Rockefeller Archive Center in Pocantico Hills, North Tarrytown, New York.

FURTHER READING

Bullock, Mary Brown. *An American Transplant; The Rockefeller Foundation and Peking Union Medical College*. Berkley: University of California Press, 1980.

Chase, Mary Ellen. *Abby Aldrich Rockefeller*. New York: Macmillan, 1950.

Collier, Peter, and David Horowitz. *The Rockefellers: An American Dynasty*. New York: Holt, Rinehart and Winston, 1976.

Corner, George W. *A History of the Rockefeller Institute, 1901–1953: Origins and Growth*. New York: The Rockefeller Institute Press, 1964.

Ferguson, Mary E. *China Medical Board and Peking Union Medical College, A Chronicle of Fruitful Collaboration*. New York: China Medical Board of New York, Inc., 1970.

Flynn, John T. *God's Gold: The Story of Rockefeller and His Times*. New York: Harcourt, Brace, 1932

Fosdick, Raymond B. *The Story of the Rockefeller Foundation*. New York: Harper and Brothers, 1952.

———. *John D. Rockefeller, Jr., A Portrait*. New York: Harper and Brothers, 1956.

———. *Adventure in Giving: The Story of the General Education Board*. New York: Harper and Row, 1962.

Gates, Frederick T. *Chapters in My Life*. New York: The Free Press, 1977.

Gibb, George Sweet, and E. H. Knowleton. *The Resurgent Years: History of the Standard Oil Company (New Jersey) 1911–1927*. New York: Harper and Brothers, 1955.

Goulder, Grace. *John D. Rockefeller, The Cleveland Years*. Cleveland: Western Reserve Historical Society, 1972.

Harr, John Ensor, and Peter J. Johnson. *The Rockefeller Century*. New York: Charles Scribner's Sons, 1988.

Hawke, David Freeman. *John D.: The Founding Father of the Rockefellers*. New York: Harper and Row, 1980.

Hidy, Ralph, and Muriel E. Hidy. *Pioneering in Big Business: History of the Standard Oil Company (New Jersey), 1882–1911.* New York: Harper and Brothers, 1955.

Johnson, Arthur M. *Winthrop W. Aldrich: Lawyer, Banker, Diplomat.* Boston: Harvard University Press, 1968.

Josephson, Matthew. *The Robber Barons.* New York: Harcourt, Brace and Company, 1938.

Krinsky, Carol Herselle. *Rockefeller Center.* New York: Oxford University Press, 1978.

McGovern, George S., and Leonard Gutteridge. *The Great Coalfield War.* Boston: Houghton Mifflin, 1972.

Nevins, Allan. *John D. Rockefeller: The Heroic Age of American Enterprise.* New York: Charles Scribner's Sons, 1940.

———. *Study in Power: John D. Rockefeller, Industrialist and Philanthropist.* New York: Charles Scribner's Sons, 1953.

Oakhill, Emily, and Kenneth W. Rose. *A Guide to Archives and Manuscripts at the Rockefeller Archive Center.* Pocantico Hills, North Tarrytown, N.Y.: Rockefeller Archive Center, 1989.

Roberts, Ann Rockefeller. *Mr. Rockefeller's Roads. The Untold Story of Acadia's Carriage Roads and Their Creator.* Camden, Me.: Down East Books, 1990.

Rockefeller, John D. *Random Reminiscences of Men and Events.* New York: Doubleday. 1908; reprinted by Fordham University Press, 1991.

Storr, Richard J. *Harper's University: The Beginnings.* Chicago: University of Chicago Press, 1966.

Tarbell, Ida M. *History of the Standard Oil Company.* New York: Phillips, 1904.

INDEX